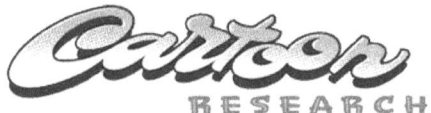

Presents

THE HARE RAISING TALES OF
CRUSADER RABBIT

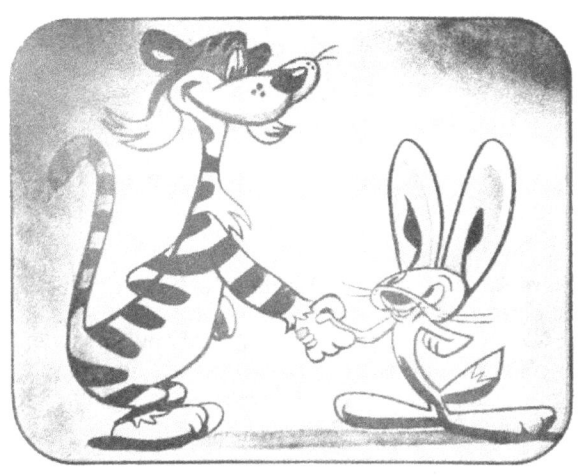

By Kevin Scott Collier

THE HARE RAISING TALES OF
CRUSADER RABBIT

By Kevin Scott Collier

Presented by

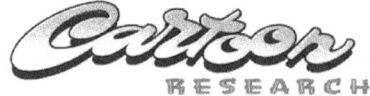

827 North Hollywood Way #100

Burbank, California 91505

Visit us online:

www.cartoonresearch.com

Founder: Jerry Beck

Email: jerrybeck18@gmail.com

This book is dedicated to
Alexander Hume Anderson Jr.

Recognition of a Historic Figure

This is my 13th title in the Cartoon Research mini-book series for Jerry Beck, and I can honestly say it is the most personal to me. As a cartoonist and illustrator, I have witnessed many examples in my life where those who have the money and authority—the hotshots that run things—exploit talent to their benefit.

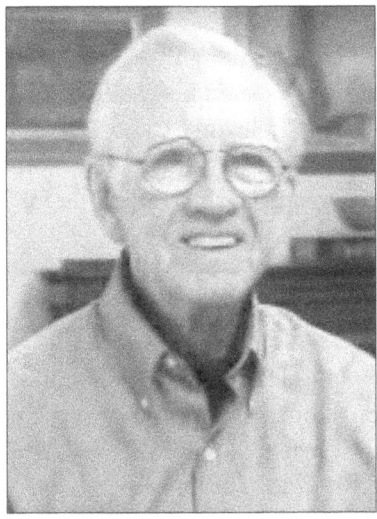

Alex Anderson, during his 2001 interview for the Television Academy Foundation.

They even steal your ideas, which has happened to me via a cartoon-character based TV show series I was involved in several years ago. The producer put his name on everything I had created, tweaking it ever so slightly to claim it as his own creation. Luckily for me, the whole thing exploded, and the 26 episodes shot never saw a broadcast.

This book is about the character *Crusader Rabbit*, but more so, about its creator, Alexander Hume Anderson, Jr. I can honestly say, in my opinion, Anderson is the most underrated, unrecognized figure in the history of television animation.

I make that statement regarding the general public and among cartoon fans. Diehard animation historians know all about Anderson, and his incredible contributions to the industry.

Anderson was a victim of unscrupulous practices that ran rampant in the era he was creating entertainment. Back then, the creative and talented people rarely had control or authority over their work. The folks who had the money did. They were businessmen, usually number crunchers and paper pushers, who looked for opportunities to make cash off the sweat and tears of others.

A couple of my Cartoon Research books addressed productions coming out of Terrytoons, and Bill Weiss kept coming up. Gene Deitch was more blunt concerning Weiss, but big deal. The truth is just what it is. And Ralph Bakshi said he liked Bill, but I could tell it was respectful

3

politeness for a dead man.

I often think if animators back then were simply paid an amount equal to the level of incompetence of their bosses, they would have all been rich.

Thus is the case of businessman-scavenger, Shull Bonsall. This man produced the second series of *Crusader Rabbit* cartoons, in color, without any involvement from Alex Anderson, or his partner, Jay Ward.

Bonsall essentially acquired *Crusader Rabbit* in a hostile takeover using the courts and his money to his advantage. That is covered in this book. But emotions aside, I like the second series of Crusader. Not as much as the first, but I think some of the critics target it because Bonsall produced it.

After Jay Ward passed away in 1989, Anderson sued his estate to recover full credit of being the creator of Rocky, Bullwinkle, and Dudley Do-Right. Ward didn't steal the characters—Anderson was being paid for their use—but his former partner was registering the copyrights for the characters in his name only.

Sadly, the general public, for the most part, didn't learn this until Anderson's death in 2010, when hundreds of newspapers published his obituary with the headline, "Creator of Rocky and Bullwinkle dies."

In researching Alexander Hume Anderson, Jr., I found a diamond among the key creators in the animation industry. One only need to view his nearly 2 and a half hour interview presented by *The Television Academy Foundation* on their website to agree. The interview, conducted by Karen Herman at his Pebble Beach, California home on July 20, 2001, is amazing. Some information from that interview contributed to this published tribute to Mr. Anderson.

Keith Scott's book, *The Moose That Roared*, also provided corroboration concerning key dates. It is an essential book for anyone who is an animation historian, or loves the world of Jay Ward productions.

Fred Patten's excellent 1982 Comics Scene articles, as well as trade magazines, entertainment periodicals, the Library of Congress archives and many or the actual cartoons to view were contributing resources.

Alex imagined a way to make original cartoons for TV. His inspiration for limited animation opened the door for many that came after.

Anderson was a true TV animation pioneer. It is my prayer this book will serve to further foster recognition of Mr. Anderson's achievements. I certainly appreciate his work, and will always admire how a relatively quiet man created such a loud movement.

- *Kevin Collier*

CHAPTER ONE

The Animation Apprentice

Alexander Hume Anderson, Jr., the creator of *Crusader Rabbit*, was born on September 5, 1920, in Berkeley, California. He was named after his father, Alexander Anderson, whom people called Sandy. Anderson's mother, Olga Terry, was the sister of Paul Terry, the founder of Terrytoons animation studio.

As a youngster, Alexander liked to paint and draw. He mainly had an interest in drawing cartoons, and silly things. He took some art lessons. Talent ran in the family. His Uncle John Terry created and produced the comic strip *Scorchy Smith,* and his Aunt Carrie Donnelly was an accomplished sculpture artist.

On his tenth birthday, Alex Anderson began a life-long friendship with a neigh-borhood boy named Joseph Ward Cohen Jr., later known as Jay Ward. Anderson, whose family was enduring hard financial times, was allowed to invite one guest over for his birthday dinner. He invited Ward. The two, who were classmates, attend-ing the same grammar and high school.

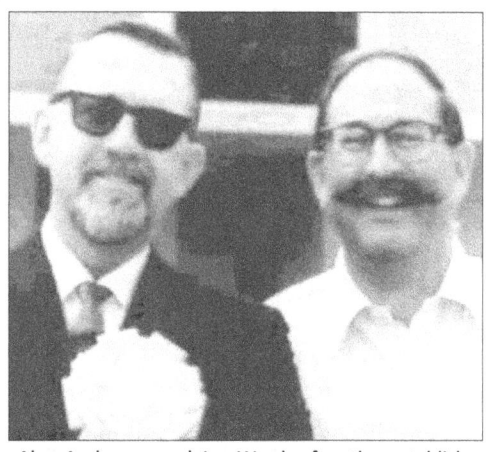

Alex Anderson and Jay Ward, after the establish-ment of Jay Ward's animation studio.

At the age of 13, Anderson's Uncle Paul Terry entertained the notion of introducing him into his studio. Uncle Paul showed him around the studio, but Alex wasn't hired into the business until after graduating from high school in 1937.

During their high school years, Anderson and Jay Ward ran several businesses together, including selling Christmas trees. Their ability to work as a team later set the animation history ball rolling.

After completing high school, Paul Terry gave his nephew a job in New York at Terrytoons. He set Anderson up in a basement apartment in Greenwich Village with two or three other artists employed at the studio. At the time, the Terrytoons Studio was located at 125th Street in

New York City.

When Anderson worked there later as an adult, the business expanded and relocated to New Rochelle.

Anderson recalled during his eight-month duration at Terrytoons that the studio was turning out 26 cartoons a year. His uncle reminded him that Walt Disney was "the Tiffany" of cartoons, but Terrytoons was "the Woolworths."

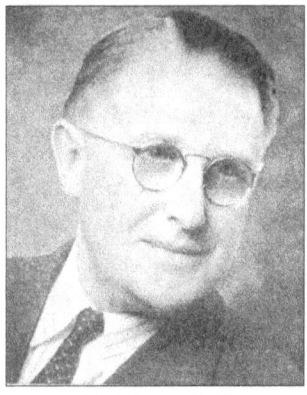

Paul Terry, 1945.

John Foster, employed in the story department, worked closely with Anderson during his entry-level year. Anderson appreciated the perspective, concluding that being on the creation end presented an opportunity to contribute something. It wasn't like being just an illustrator replicating someone else's idea.

Uncle Paul switched Anderson between departments to learn all aspects of cartoon production, including operating the animation camera.

Departing Terrytoons, Anderson returned to Berkeley to attend college at the University of California, Berkeley. Jay Ward had enrolled there a year earlier. The two became fraternity brothers and orchestrated activities on campus and organized a basketball team.

Back in business as partners, the pair made an arrangement with the college art and music shop to offer the latest hit records at a discount to fraternities and sororities.

The hit parade venture didn't make much money, but it did provide a way to meet new friends, especially girls.

After graduating in 1942, Anderson attended the California School of Fine Arts, but dropped out due to America's entry into World War II. Anderson enlisted in the United States Navy, where he served for 3 1/2 years. Afterward, he resumed his job at Terrytoons in New York, putting in a couple of years there.

While working on *Mighty Mouse*, and other cartoons, Anderson was inspired to create one of his own. Finding it amusing that a mouse could fly, Anderson imag-

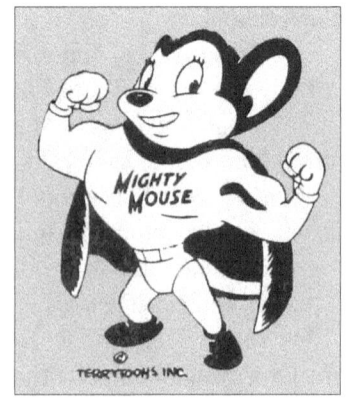

Mighty Mouse.

6

ined, *Why not a squirrel?* Some of them can fly. The genesis of Rocky also included a back-woods moose as a companion. It all pretty much remained in his imagination, until partnering with Jay Ward in 1948 to establish Television Arts Productions, Inc. Much like Bullwinkle pulled "a rabbit out of a hat," Anderson tapped into the ideas when the new studio engaged in creating a demo reel of cartoons to find a network buyer.

The original idea for Rocky, the flying squirrel, had the rodent wearing manufactured wings that enabled him to fly.

Anderson even found a name for the moose, Bullwinkle, named after Clarence Ahrens Bullwinkel. The real-deal was a branch manager and salesman for a Berkeley Ford automobile dealership.

But this isn't about a moose and squirrel, it's about a jackrabbit and tiger.

Before departing Terrytoons in early 1948, Anderson approached his Uncle Paul with the idea for an animated cartoon series for television.

That idea would be the first made-for-television animated cartoon series. Even though Uncle Paul turned it down.

CHAPTER TWO

The Origin of Crusader Rabbit

One of the most informative resources concerning the creation of *Crusader Rabbit* is an interview with Alex Anderson presented by *The Television Academy Foundation*. In it, he also explains his vision of "limited animation," the process that allowed original made-for-TV cartoons to be financially possible.

Karen Herman conducted the comprehensive, two-and-a-half hour interview with Anderson at his Pebble Beach, California, home on July 20, 2010. *The Television Academy Foundation* hosts the monumental video online.

In the interview, Alex Anderson explains that Crusader didn't begin as a rabbit at all.

"I wanted to create a character that followed the theme of *Don Quixote*," Anderson said. "I thought, wouldn't it be good to have a donkey, and called him Donkey Hote. And have another character who would play the role of Sancho Panza."

Paul Terry had offered the resources of his studio to his ambitious nephew to develop his vision for a television cartoon.

Donkeys and mules didn't have a track record in animation for being heroes. The first of merit in animated cartoons was *Maud the Mule*, a creation of comic strip artist Frederick Opper.

The series, which made its debut in 1916 via International Film Service, presented a revenge-seeking mule who liked to kick his owner, farmer Si Slocum, into the air. Subsequently, animated depictions of

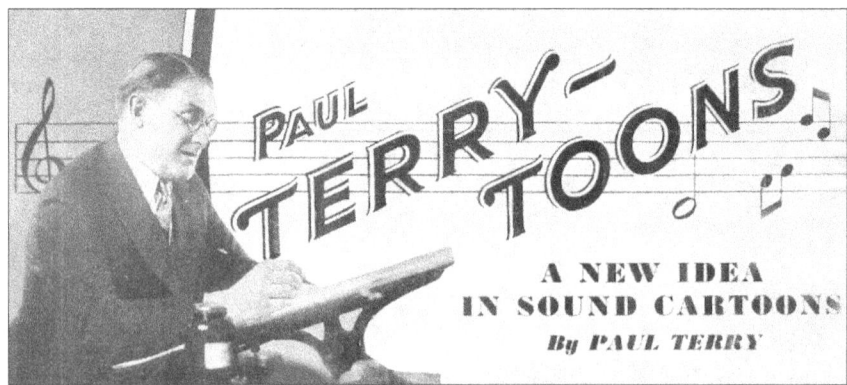

1947 magazine advertisement for Terrytoons, featuring Paul Terry.

donkeys and mules relegated them to unintelligent, hillbilly-like status.

Anderson gathered up his donkey sketches and brought them to Terrytoons illustrator Arthur Bartsch, seeking his opinion. Bartsch, who primarily drew backgrounds for Terrytoons, and illustrated Terrytoons comic books for St. John Publishing, also developed models of characters seen in studio productions.

What transpired during their meeting places Bartsch as a link in the chain leading to the creation of Anderson's fearless hare.

"Artie Bartsch, the model designer for Terrytoons, said 'I really don't think that a donkey is a good character. Why don't you do a little rabbit?'" Anderson recalled during his interview with *The Television Academy Foundation*. "So, I thought, maybe a rabbit."

Anderson wanted to pair the rabbit with an unlikely, contrasting partner. He imagined a tiger, but concluded that presenting the animals with their traditional temperaments would be unamusing. Perhaps a tiger that didn't have the temperament of one would work.

"My thought was to have a rabbit, and a tiger, but to switch their personalities. The rabbit would be the aggressive tiger-like character, and the tiger could be more of a gentle soul. So, it would be kind of a switch. And it was the essence that I approached Uncle Paul with."

A jackrabbit appearance developed, which added spunk to the demeanor of the character. The tall, upright ears also created a confidence factor, allowing the rabbit to appear to stand taller than he actually was.

Anderson had acquired a fondness for child actor Jackie "Butch" Jenkins, and borrowed from his appearance. Jenkins had recently received star billing in MGM's *Boys' Ranch* motion picture. The comical, freckle-faced, toothy kid figured into the developing features of Crusader.

The heroic hare apparently languished without a designated name until Anderson reconnected with Jay Ward to establish Television Arts Productions, Inc. in May of 1948. According to Anderson, Jay Ward suggested the title for the show, *Crusader Rabbit*, thus giving the feisty little fighter a moniker.

When Television Arts Productions hired a staff, which began working on the first *Crusader Rabbit* animations, Gerald Ray became another link in the development of the character's appearance.

Ray modified, polished and refined the final appearance of *Crusader Rabbit*, much to Anderson's approval.

The jovial tiger subsequently became known as Ragland T. Tiger, or "Rags" for short. The name originated from the jazz composition, *Tiger Rag*, composed by the Original Dixieland Jazz Band in 1917. The composition is often put to use as a fighting theme by collegiate and professional sports teams with a tiger mascot.

Creating characters is one thing, requiring an investment of time and creativity. Producing an original cartoon series exclusively made for television would be an expensive prospect. Anderson knew that the full-animation techniques used in theatrical films made the notion prohibitive. But his intrigue with the new medium of television, and something he had seen in a Disney production preview of a *Baby Weems* cartoon, compelled him to pursue the goal.

Anderson recalled with fascination the first time he saw a television set. It was with his uncle when he came home after his naval service.

"When I went back [home] right after the war, my Uncle [Paul] met me at the train, and we stopped by [the home of] Clarence Menser, who was the vice-president [of programming] at NBC. He had a beautiful TV set," Anderson recalled in his *TTAF* interview. "When I saw that, I thought, *This is a new world*. That is when the thought occurred to me it would be a new world for animation. I thought I would do it for my uncle [at Terrytoons]. [But] 20th Century Fox saw television as the great threat to their whole world."

After working with Arthur Bartsch, Anderson pitched the *Crusader Rabbit* TV show to Paul Terry. He turned it down.

"He said, 'If you want to do this,' he suggested, 'I do it on my own,'" Anderson said. "He added, 'Just don't tell anybody who is your uncle.'"

Anderson subsequently learned it was nothing personal, nor was it a rejection of the characters, or series idea. It all had to do with business. 20th Century Fox, Terrytoon's distributor, saw television as the enemy. Theatrical cartoon studios were warned to stay away from television production by their distributors, or face cancellation of their contracts. No distributor, no Terrytoons.

But Anderson continued to imagine a pathway of bringing his original cartoon series to television.

Inspiring Anderson to proceed was something he saw years earlier in the Disney film, *The Reluctant Dragon*.

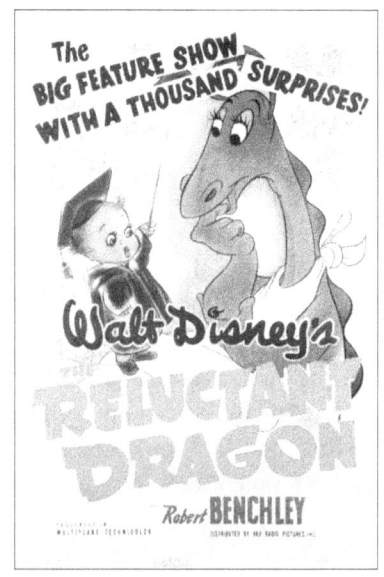

The Reluctant Dragon poster, 1941.

"As a part of it, there was a sequence where Bob Benchley goes behind the scenes in the story department with art lined up on the wall," Anderson recalled.

Robert Benchley, a popular radio comedian, starred in the feature film, which was basically a presentation featuring Disney's new animation studio facility in Burbank, California.

In a sequence, Benchley learns about the animation process in a preview for the production of a *Baby Weems* cartoon.

"That was a case where they just had stills, and a little lip action, so there could be some movement," he recalled. "I came away from that, and thought, really, that was every bit as interesting as the fully animated *The Reluctant Dragon*. I felt at that point, yes, this is going to be a new world for animation."

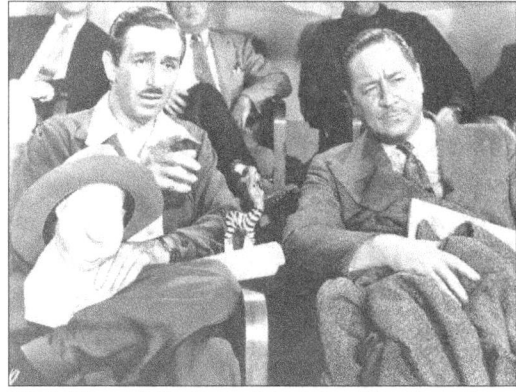

Walt Disney, left, shows Robert Benchley the animation process in a projection room, 1941.

What Anderson envisioned was "limited animation," which provided an answer to the technical and economical entry of original cartoon programs for television.

Anderson believed getting in on the ground floor of television was important, but saw it was perhaps too early, as there wasn't the money to accomplish it all. Sponsors were just warming up to television, but investment was spotty.

Anderson left Terrytoons and New Rochelle, New York, and headed back to Berkeley with the idea of establishing a studio. To get the ball rolling on turning *Crusader Rabbit* into a cartoon for TV, Anderson reached out to his old pal, Jay Ward. With Ward onboard, Anderson imagined his partner could handle the business end, while he tended to the ideas, art, and animation side.

On July 26, 1948, Alex Anderson and Jay Ward opened a temporary office for their new company, Television Arts Productions, Inc., renting space, several floors up, at NBC central, 111 Sutter Street, in Berkeley. In short order, they relocated, moving TAP to 2733 Stuart Street. Their new headquarters was garage behind the home of Anderson's parents. They converted the area into an office space and studio.

Coming up with a 15-minute preview reel featuring three distinct cartoon segment samples, TAP arranged an October meeting at NBC headquarters in New York. Jay Ward presented the "pilot" for a proposed series, *The Comic Strips for Television,* to NBC's director of programming, Russell Johnson. The trio of short tales introduced *Crusader Rabbit, Dudley Doright* (the original spelling), and *Hamhock Jones.*

The network passed on all but one of the characters featured: *Crusader Rabbit.* Anderson's favorite in the batch, *Hamhock Jones,* didn't make the final cut. The proposed series starred a private detective who had Siamese twins to care for, one good, the other bad.

Johnson put TAP in touch with Jerry Fairbanks, whose company was under an exclusive contract to provide the network with all of its new television programs.

Jerry Fairbanks wasn't just an opportunist, or a nobody. He was *the guy* supplying NBC with all of its new shows. His resume was impressive, and exceptional.

In 1945, Fairbanks won the Academy Award for Best Short Subject, One Reel category, for *Who's Who in Animal Land,* while working at Paramount. Three years later he was nominated again in that category for *Moon Rockets.*

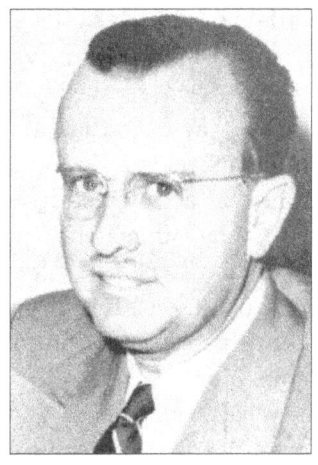

Jerry Fairbanks.

Also in 1945, Fairbanks had established Jerry Fairbanks, Inc., a studio that produced industrial films. *Variety* announced on February 26, 1946, Fairbank's early leap into producing programs specifically for TV. Fairbanks' move took place before television sets were available to the public, "Jumping the gun on television receiver manufacturers who don't expect to begin marketing sets before summer," *Variety* reported. "United States Television Manufacturing expects to have a line of video sets in stores by early May."

The price of sets didn't turn Fairbanks away, either. A 16 x 24 inch set was expected to retail for $900, the equivalent of over $12,000 today.

"Jerry Fairbanks set a deal here with NBC for the production of television films for the network," *Variety* said. "Fairbanks will [also] continue to make film shorts for Paramount."

But not for much longer.

Paramount served Fairbanks with an ultimatum. Drop TV or we drop you. It was the same position Paul Terry was familiar with. Production for theaters and television don't mix.

Fairbanks quit Paramount, and quickly moved up the ranks at NBC.

Sponsor magazine reported Jerry Fairbanks, Inc. was "the first Hollywood film organization to produce films especially for TV."

With a thumbs up from NBC to proceed with the *Crusader Rabbit* series, Television Arts Productions, Inc. hired a small staff for starters to produce five initial chapters of what would become the jackrabbit's series debut adventure, *Crusader Rabbit vs. the State of Texas.*

The first employee TAP hired was former Disney animator Gerry Ray.

"I was the first guy who ever went to work for Jay and Alex," Ray stated *Comics Scene*, in 1982. "They got another fellow, Bob Mills, who was an inker. We drew on illustration board, and then Bob would do the inking and put tone on it. Then they got a fellow named Tom Stanford to run the camera."

TAP completed production on the first five *Crusader Rabbit* short reels in January 1949. Jerry Fairbanks officially announced the *Crusader Rabbit* series to the media on the 19th of that month.

Motion Picture Daily reported on the announcement the next day in its pages.

"The first mass production of cartoons filmed especially for television was revealed here today [January 19] when Jerry Fairbanks Productions scheduled for immediate shooting a series of 130 animated video shorts," *Motion Picture Daily* reported. "The filming of the series will be done by a newly-developed television animation

TV CARTOONS

Fairbanks Plans Series

FIRST large scale production of cartoon films designed for television has been announced by Jerry Fairbanks Productions. Plans call for 130 animated open-end five minute shorts.

Based upon a continuing story premise, series will be offered to television stations singly as well as local, regional and national advertisers. At start series will consist of daily show for 26 weeks.

Animation for *Crusader Rabbit*, as the series will be known, is to be done by Television Arts Productions, Berkeley, Calif. The firm was recently organized by J. Troplong Ward, San Francisco radio producer, and Alexander Anderson, former animator and story editor of Terrytoons. Films are to be completed at the Fairbanks studios where editing and voice dubbing, narration and scoring will be added.

Newly developed Teletoons animation technique, according to Mr. Fairbanks, eliminates many of the costly features of theatrical animation while retaining illusion of movement and life. To accomplish this, Mr. Fairbanks says that backgrounds are held to a minimum and closeups featured. This method cuts cost sharply, he feels.

Broadcast article, January 24, 1950.

technique by Television Arts Productions, a Berkeley firm organized recently by Alexander Anderson, a former animator for Terrytoons, and J. Troplong Ward, a San Francisco producer."

Broadcast magazine published details of the Fairbanks/TAP arrangement and plans in its January 24 edition.

"The cartoon series, based upon the continuing story premise, will consist of a daily show for 26 weeks," *Broadcast* reported. "Animation for *Crusader Rabbit*, as the series will be known, is to be done by Television Arts Productions, Berkeley, California, recently organized by J. Troplong Ward, San Francisco radio producer, and Alexander Anderson, a former animator and story editor at Terrytoons."

Broadcast explained the films shot at TAP would "be completed at the Fairbanks Studios, where editing and voice dubbing, narration and scoring will be added."

Broadcast reported a newly developed "Teletoons" animation technique, which, "according to Mr. Fairbanks, eliminates many of the costly features of theatrical animation while retaining the illusion of movement and life."

"To accomplish this, Mr. Fairbanks says that backgrounds are held to a minimum and close-ups featured," *Broadcast* reported. "This method cuts cost sharply, he feels."

NBC's interest in *Crusader Rabbit* suddenly evaporated when they previewed the completed five chapters that January. It wasn't all they had imagined.

With the films being so short, and having to be parceled out, NBC decided it wasn't worth the hassle to try to schedule them. Nor did they see an opportunity to make adequate revenue considering all the time and investment involved. As a result, *Crusader Rabbit* wasn't going to be broadcast nationally over the network.

News of NBC throwing *Crusader Rabbit* under the bus was first re-

Inside Television

NBC has turned down Jerry Fairbanks Production's "Crusader Rabbit" television series. Pact between producer and net gives web first refusal on all vidpix turned out by Fairbanks concern. As a result of the NBC snub, Fairbanks will peddle the pix himself. The films are five-minute animated shorts. Firm will make 130 reels and offer them to video outlets.

Variety article, February 2, 1950. NBC turns down the option to bring *Crusader Rabbit* to network television.

ported by *Variety* in its February 2 edition.

"NBC has turned down Jerry Fairbanks Productions' *Crusader Rabbit* television series," it reported. "As a result of the NBC snub, Fairbanks will peddle the pictures himself."

Fairbanks' contract with NBC provided an option that allowed him to independently distribute the series himself. However, it also meant NBC wouldn't be paying Fairbanks to make the series. And in turn, Fairbanks wouldn't be funded to pay TAP to create it.

Fairbanks knew that to keep the ball rolling he had to raise capital. And to raise money, he also had to raise interest. The salesman in him went into overdrive. Fairbanks wasn't going to give up on *Crusader*.

Variety reported on February 8 that *Crusader Rabbit* would be offered for sale to "stations and advertisers at one of the lowest prices yet for pictures made especially for TV."

Variety explained the cost for per station would range from $75 to $150, depending on the size of the market area and number of homes with receivers.

"Fairbanks was able to bring the films in at cost permitting the low rentals through use of a new simulated animation system, in which much of the animation is effected through varying camera angles, with a minimum amount of actual animation."

Telecasting magazine, along with many more, climbed aboard the *Crusader Rabbit* publicity train for months. Fairbanks increased the publicity by hosting a *Crusader Rabbit* preview party, inviting the members of the press and their children. It received much fanfare, and the event included a large stage featuring a merry-go-round.

With the buzz he created, and interest expressed through media coverage, Fairbanks confidently approached NBC in order to borrow some money to fully engage production of the *Crusader Rabbit* series. Reliant on Fairbanks as their sole new content provider, they agreed to the loan.

Variety reported in its September 7 issue that full production of the *Crusader Rabbit* series had received the green light.

"Jerry Fairbanks goes into production with the *Crusader Rabbit* television series this week," *Variety* announced. "Fairbanks will can a 13-week group of 65 pictures. The animation is being done by Television Arts Productions, of Berkeley. Dubbing, narration, editing and scoring will be handled at Fairbank's plant."

Crusader Rabbit, the character Alex Anderson affectionately said was "two-and-a-half carrots tall," was now officially on his way to television.

CHAPTER THREE

The First Crusader Rabbit Series

The first series of *Crusader Rabbit* cartoons, filmed in black and white, was comprised of 195 five-minute chapters, spread over ten distinct adventures.

Jerry Fairbanks, Inc., served as executive producer of the series, with Television Arts Productions, Inc., Alex Anderson and Jay Ward as producers. TAP held the copyright on the show.

Jerry Fairbanks, Inc. financed the production of the cartoons and represented Crusader Rabbit as its distributor, selling the series to television stations around the country.

The financial agreement between Fairbanks and Television Arts Productions, signed on October 4, 1950, called for Anderson and Ward to receive 50% of the profits.

Salesman Jerry Fairbanks had a habit of issuing press releases identifying stations expressing interest in the series before actual contracts were signed representing a sale. The practice left an impression *Crusader Rabbit* was first broadcast on television as early as September 1,

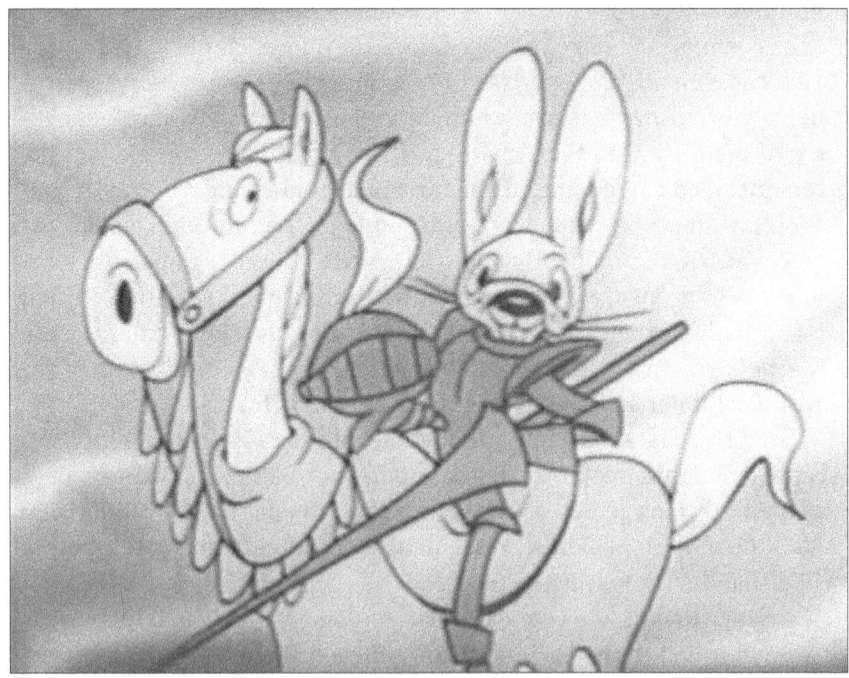

Crusader Rabbit animated series opening sequence illustrated by Alex Anderson.

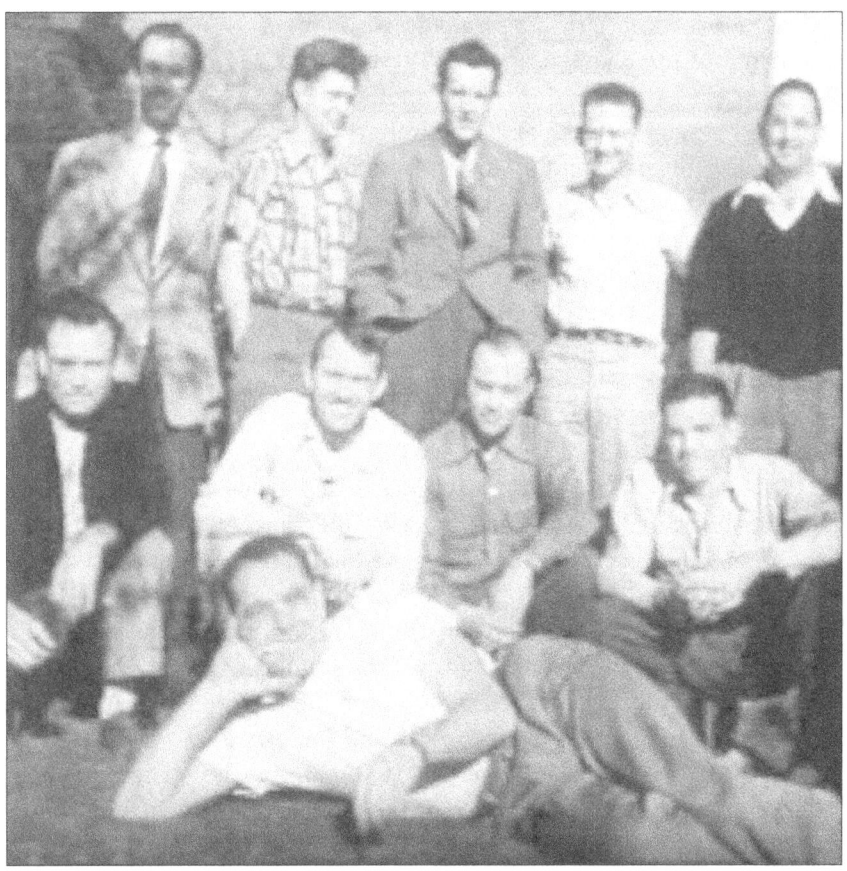

Early Television Arts Productions, Inc. staff. Top row, far right, Jay Ward. Kneeling row, Alex Anderson, second from the left.

1949. Production of the cartoon was underway at the time, but the show didn't debut until August 1, 1950, via station KNBH in Los Angeles.

The first series wasn't completed at the time of its premiere, either. The first set of 65 chapters began production the first week of September 1949. Another 65 were finished the following year. A final set of 65 chapters were completed in 1951.

Before the hare-brained series, Television Arts Productions, Inc. had produced a 15-minute pilot, *The Comic Strips for Television*. Besides *Crusader Rabbit*, the presentation piece featured *Dudley Doright* and *Hamhock Jones*. The first chapter of the series adventure *Crusader Rabbit vs. the State of Texas* originated from this demo reel.

The Comic Strips for Television pilot was created prior to TAP possessing a working staff of employees. Alex Anderson and Jay Ward created the film entirely by themselves.

17

The series title, *Crusader Rabbit*, also the name of the character, was suggested by Jay Ward for the creation of the pilot.

The partnership established with Jerry Fairbanks provided funding for Television Arts Productions, Inc., enabling Anderson and Ward to hire a staff.

Anderson's connections in the animation industry via Terrytoons brought in many established cartoon professionals. Sometimes curious talents dropped by the studio to see what was going on and ended up working on an adventure or two.

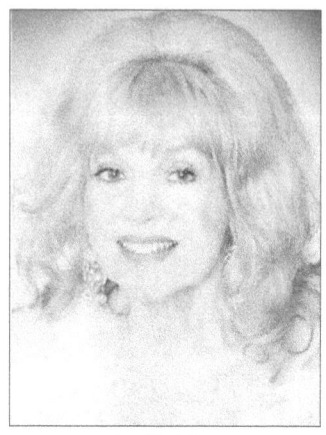
Lucille Bliss.

Writers of the *Crusader Rabbit* series included Joe Curtin, Hal Goodman, Arthur North, Lloyd Turner, Jack Miller, and Alex Anderson, who overseeing on all scripts. Jay Ward provided some writing and editing of the *Crusader Rabbit* stories. Anderson also frequently directed.

Joseph Curtin, a Canadian illustrator, previously had worked with Terrytoons. Curtin developed many of the supporting series characters. Lloyd Turner subsequently became a prominent writer for Jay Ward's animated cartoon production of *Rocky and Bullwinkle and Friends*.

San Francisco business owner Wayne Stahmer, who operated Sound Recorders, suggested the names of individuals who might be a good match as character voices in the series. Jay Ward cast the voice actors, and oversaw the sound production of dialogue, which was recorded at Stahmer's studio.

The main voice artists hired included announcer Roy Whaley, who narrated the adventures. Lucille Bliss, Vern Louden and Russ Coughlin provided the main character voices. Coughlin routinely played the villains. Tom Stanford and Patti Pritchard presented additional voices.

Lucille Bliss performed the voice of Crusader Rabbit, with Vern Louden playing Ragland T. Tiger. Russ Coughlin provided the voice of leading nemesis Dudley Nightshade, which was a predecessor to Snidely Whiplash, in the subsequent *Dudley Do-Right* cartoon series.

Artists, illustrators, and animators working on the first series included Alex Anderson, Bob Bastian, Bob Bemiller, Chuck Fusion, Randy Grochoski, Ed King, Bob Mills, Lee Mishkin, Grim Natwick, Russ Sholl, Jim Scott, John Sparey, Dean Spille, Ted Martine, Spaulding White, and Volney White.

Anderson illustrated the iconic series introduction, featuring the

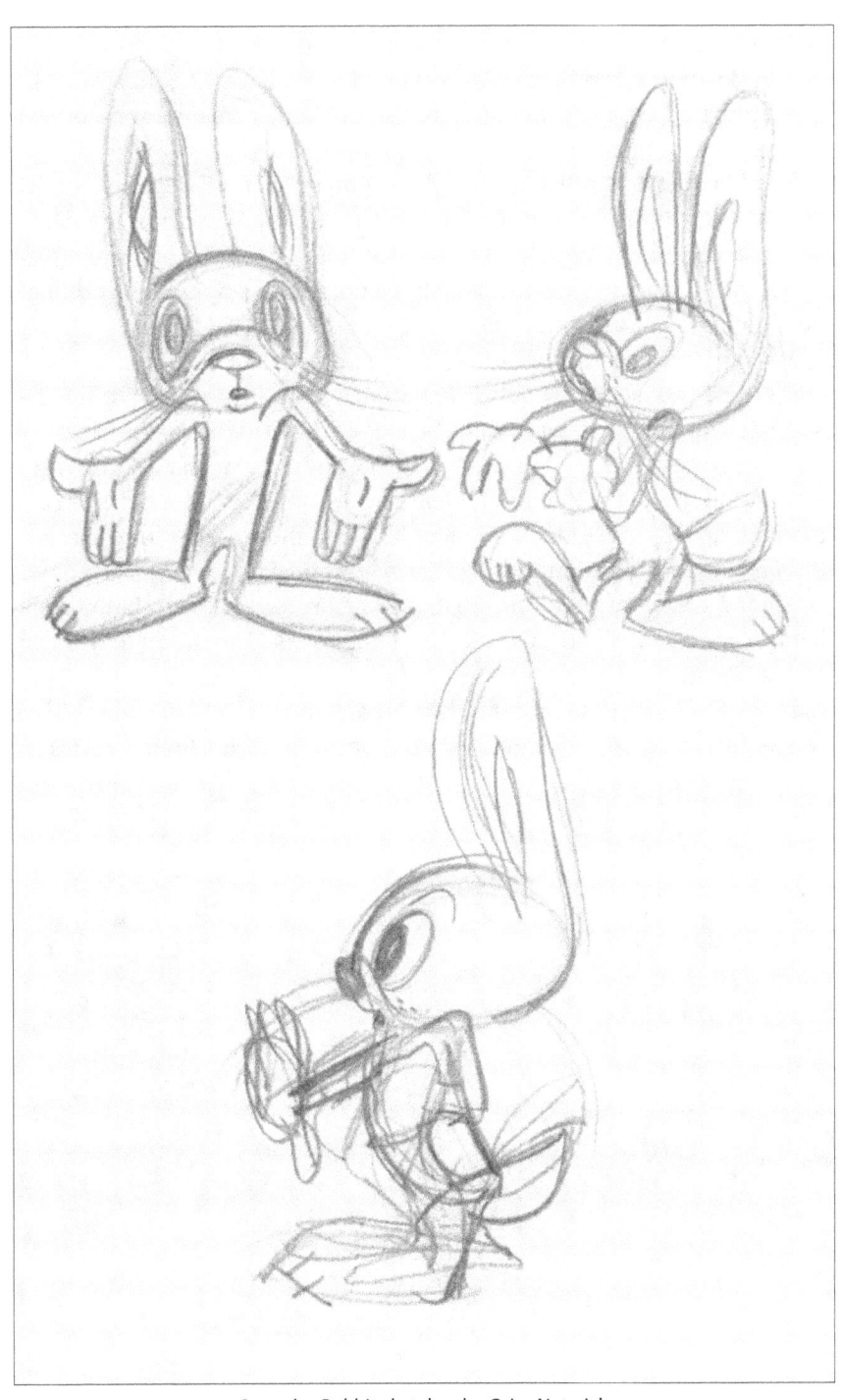

Crusader Rabbit sketches by Grim Natwick.

jackrabbit in armor riding into the scene on a horse.

Bob Bastian at the time was working as an advertising illustrator in San Francisco, and became an editorial cartoonist in 1953 for the *San Francisco Chronicle*.

Bob Bemiller had previously worked as an animator for Fleischer Studios. Subsequently, he worked for Hanna Barbera, Filmation and Marvel Productions.

Bob Mills, an aspiring cartoonist, eventually was appointed production manager in the first *Crusader Rabbit* series.

Mishkin went on to work on *King Leonardo, Calvin and the Colonel,* and *Mr. Magoo* series. He also won an Academy Award in 1970 for the animated short *Is It Always Right to be Right?* Mishkin was director.

Grim Natwick began his career in the animation business in 1917 working for William Randolph Heart's International Film Service cartoon studio. He also gained an incredible resume working for Fleischer Studio and assisted in animating Disney's *Fantasia*.

Among other things, John Sparey went on to work for Hanna Barbera, working on *Jonny Quest, The Flintstones, The Herculoids,* and *Space Ghost*.

Dean Spille was an accomplished painter and background artist, whose future credits included working on the *Charlie Brown* series of

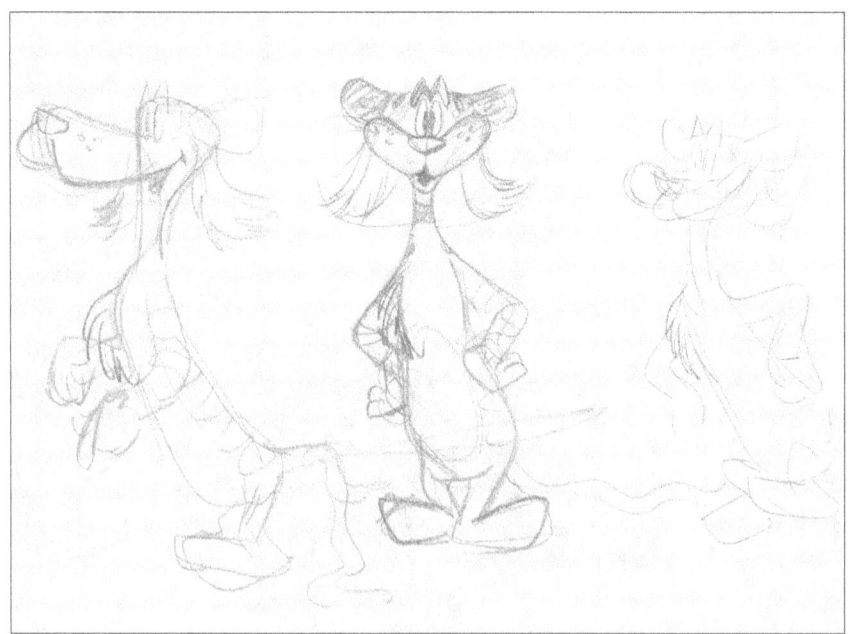

Original Ragland T. Tiger sketch by Grim Natwick.

primetime television cartoon specials. Charles Schulz' classic, *A Charlie Brown Christmas,* being the most recognizable.

Russ Sholl was a commercial illustrator. Ted Martine worked for a newspaper as an cartoonist and writer.

Spaulding White and Chuck Fusion had worked for Disney previously. Volney White had been an animator at Warner Brothers for *Looney Tunes* and *Merrie Melodies*, and was a former director at Terrytoons.

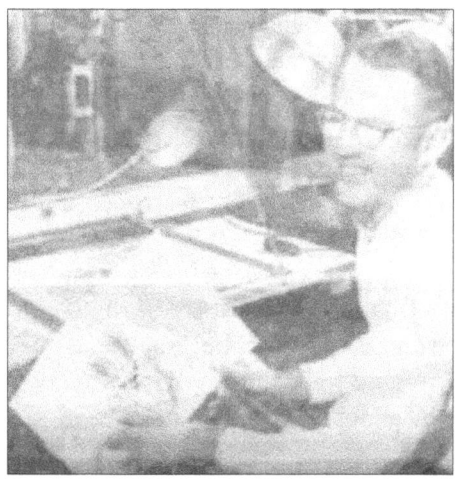
Alex Anderson drawing Crusader Rabbit at his desk at Television Arts Productions, Inc.

Bob Oleson and Jack Williams oversaw camera operations, with editing by Tom Stanford. Over a decade later, Stanford received an Academy Award for his work the film *West Side Story.*

Clarence E. Wheeler provided music for the series. The theme tune was based on the public domain children's rhyme *Ten Little Indians.*

As the flow of work grew, Television Arts Productions, Inc. expanded, too, eventually relocating their studio to Los Angeles in 1951.

In the first series adventure, *Crusader Rabbit vs. the State of Texas,* Crusader and his companion Rags journey to the Lone Star state to stop the extermination of jackrabbits—many of which are Crusader's cousins. Placed in danger by the state's policy of "hare today, gone tomorrow," Crusader faces several challenges.

The story, told in 15 chapters, introduces Crusader and Rags to television viewers, successfully defining the character of each.

We learn the jackrabbit reads and studies all matters concerning leadership, bravery, and battle. The opening scene of the adventure pictures Crusader reclining beneath an enormous toadstool reading a book about Sir Galahad. Surrounding him are books such as *Truman's Campaign, Caesar's Campaigns,* and *Napoleon's Battles.*

We discover from the outset Crusader doesn't just spring into action when a matter is of personal concern. He's a champion, advocate, and reformer for hire. Signs posted outdoors near his rabbit hole read, "Specialist all types of crusades," "Crusading rates by week or month," and, "Bargain prices to widows and orphans." A large "CR" crest is displayed mounted on a tree.

The first chapter of *Crusader Rabbit vs. the State of Texas* presents the first meeting of Ragland T. Tiger and the hare, establishing their partnership. Crusader visits the circus to recruit an assistant on his Texas adventure, and stumbles upon a "Man-Eating Tiger."

The caged beast isn't so ferocious. The roars emitted from his cage are courtesy of a sound effects record played on a Victrola. Crusader pitches his mission to the tiger, who agrees to tag along. Crusader picks the lock on his cage, releasing the tiger. And, away they go!

One enjoyable aspect in the series is the story's narrator interacting with Crusader Rabbit, Rags, and guests. The storyteller helps guide the two and frequently speaks to the two stars. Crusader routinely corrects the announcer, sometimes engaging in arguments concerning details in the story.

The pair confronts several adversaries on the way to, and inside of, Texas. Vernon the Vulture is the first. Believing the rabbit and lion will not survive their desert crossing, the bird imagines the couple as dinner. Dead-Eye Dobbins, a dastardly sharp-shooter, and his dog, confront the heroes next.

They arrive in Cactus Junction, disguised in costume as a horse. The

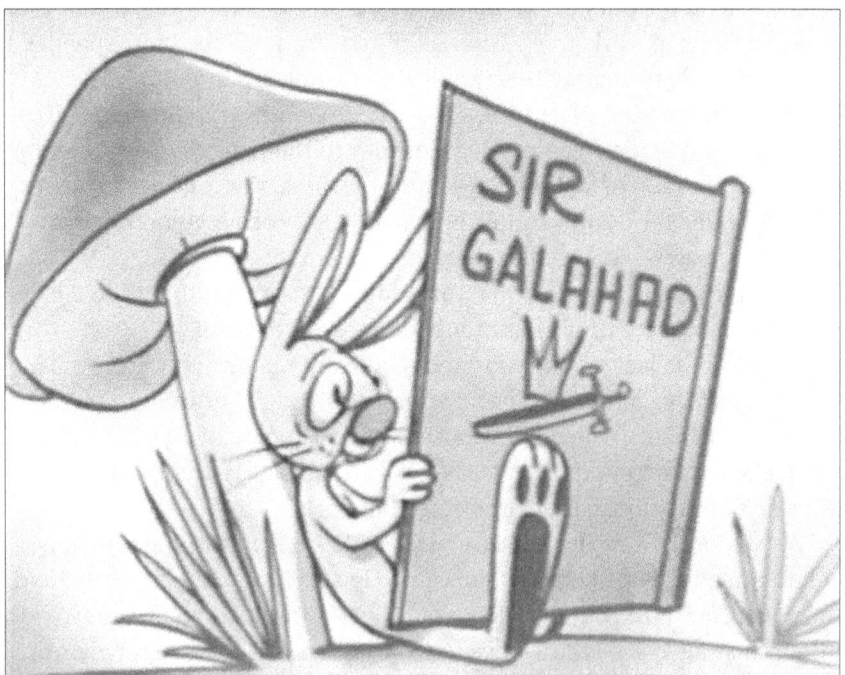

The first appearance of Crusader Rabbit in chapter one of the *Crusader Rabbit vs. the State of Texas* adventure.

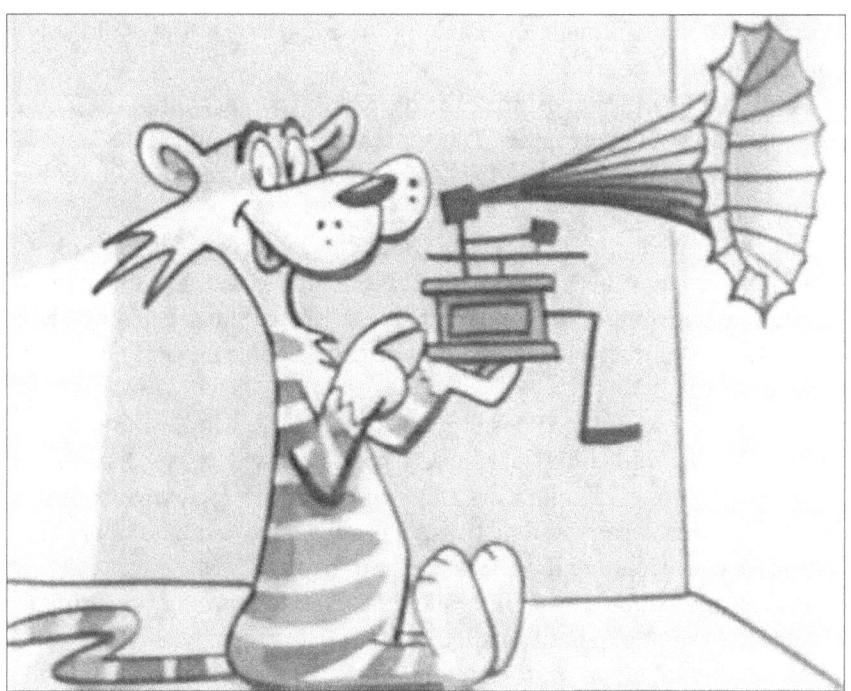

The first appearance of Crusader Rabbit in chapter one of the *Crusader Rabbit vs. the State of Texas* adventure.

small Texas town has a significant presence, a tough-guy named Granite Jaw Jones. The fearless cowpoke wears garter snakes to hold up his socks and uses an acetylene torch to shave.

Crusader and Rags mosey into the saloon. The hare jumps up onto the counter and announces, "I can lick any man at this bar." Granite's right-hand man, Spike, promptly throws the rabbit out of the establishment and into the street.

Undeterred, Crusader and Rags defeat Granite Jaw Jones and the townsfolk sign a treaty supporting the right for rabbits to exist in Texas.

Crusader and Rags travel to Dead Man's Corner, a town exploding with gunplay and lawlessness. The most prominent industries in town were the funeral parlors and undertakers. Winning over this place would take an act of God, or maybe the weather.

After their arrival, and Crusader has served notice on the gunslingers, a Texas twister barrels through the town leaving destruction and fear in its path. The bad guys think the ruin was caused by the rabbit, and surrender, signing the peace treaty.

Crusader and Rags move on, continuing their mission to reverse the statewide rabbit ban. But liberating hares one town at a time seems impossible. Thus, Crusader thinks taking the issue to the top would solve the dilemma in one stroke.

Disguised in a horse costume, the hare and tiger sneak into the Texas State building of departments. They enter the "Rabbit and Hare Removal Department" office, where they gain access to the commissioner, big game hunter Frank Sawbuck.

Sawbuck reveals to Crusader and Rags the reason for the rabbit ban. The creatures have been eating all of the carrots in Texas, leaving none for human consumption. As a result, it has caused diminished eyesight for all Lone Star state citizens. It doesn't help that Sawbuck is also allergic to rabbits.

During their meeting, Rags stumbles out of the window, taking the horse costume with him, leaving Crusader exposed before Sawbuck's nearsighted eyes. Crusader persuades Sawbuck that he convinced rabbits to stop eating carrots. Trusting the promise, the commissioner signs the peace treaty, ending the Texas ban on rabbits.

Rags suggests that cream puffs should serve as a winning substitute to change the rabbit population's diet.

The elaborate cream puff campaign unfolds, featuring Crusader tell-

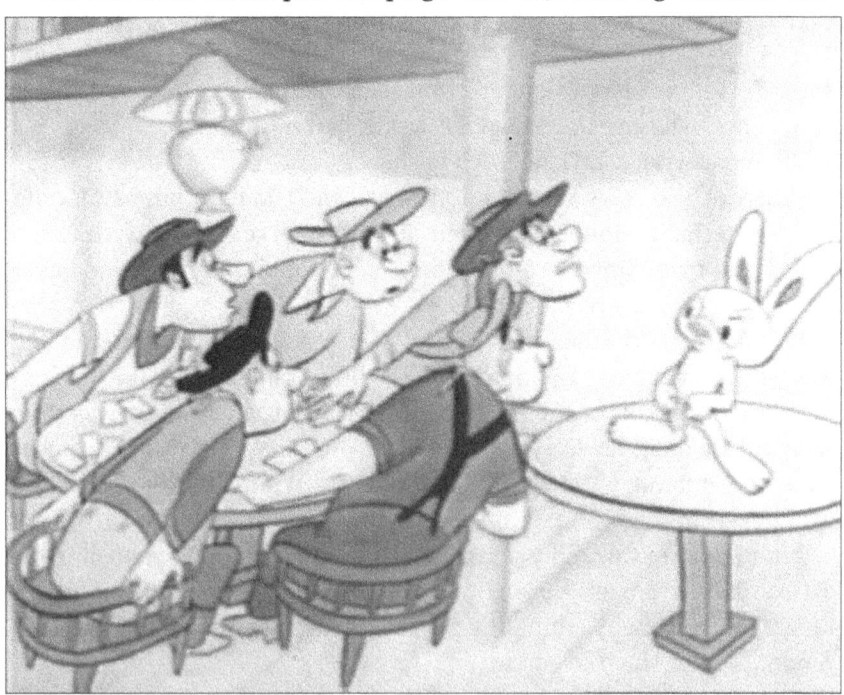

The heroic hare gets the attention of patrons in a saloon in *Crusader Rabbit vs. the State of Texas*.

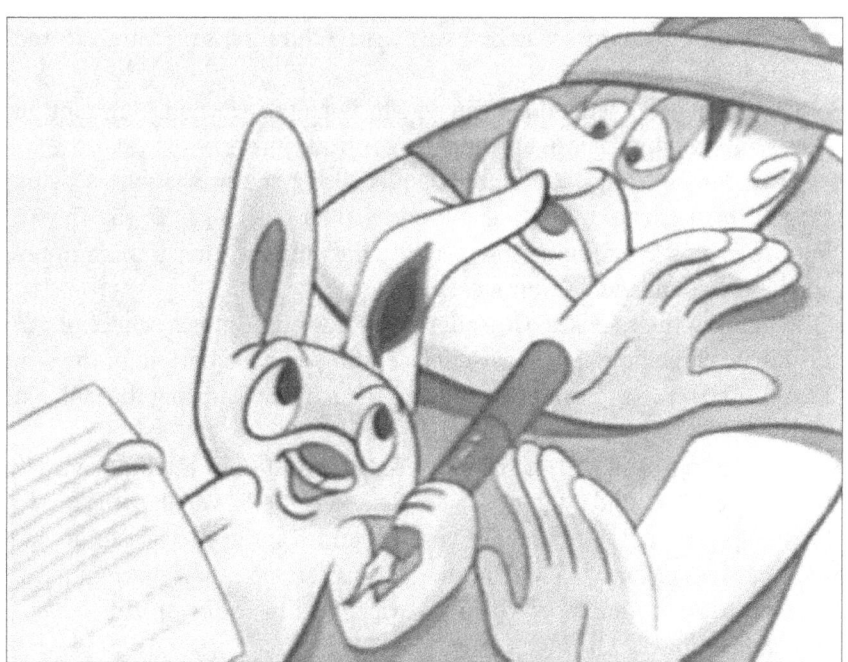

The heroic hare gets commissioner Frank Sawbuck to sign the peace treaty in *Crusader Rabbit vs. the State of Texas.*

ing a gathering of rabbits at a deportation center they can grow big and strong by consuming the treat. Rags hides inside a large rabbit costume to back up the claim.

The 15-chapter adventure ends with ten million stubborn rabbits agreeing to change their diet leaving the carrots for the consumption of Texans. Eyesight is restored and the rabbits return. Crusader is awarded a medal from Sawbuck and a statue of the heroic rabbit is erected in his honor.

Introduced at the end of chapters is a simple teaser that became a trademark amusement over a decade later in *Rocky and Bullwinkle* cartoons. The "join us next time" promo, which featured a gag, was first established in the *Crusader Rabbit* cartoon series.

In the second *Crusader Rabbit* adventure, *Crusader Rabbit vs. the Pirates*, the pair journey to the Gulf Coast for a little rest.

While fishing atop a garbage scow in a New Orleans port, the hare and tiger discover a message in a floating bottle. The note calls for help. The author of the message conveys that pirates are attacking. The note includes the precise location, in longitude and latitude.

Crusader and Rags build a sailing boat from scraps atop the scow and christens it the Robert E. Leak. They set sail to learn if the pirate threat is current, or just a message that was written hundreds of years ago and managed to survive.

They stop at a castle along the way to borrow a cannon to mount on their sailboat, just in case they indeed confront pirates.

Crusader and Rags encounter danger along the way, such as being tangled up in an old, floating minefield. The pair survives the threat, but provisions are running low, and the hot sun has caused them to become delusional and see mirages.

Regaining their senses, Crusader and Rags encounter a school of Tin Fish, who carve holes in their vessel, sending it to the bottom of the sea. Dunkin Island rises from the seabed to the surface, carrying the sailboat with it out of the water.

Finding footprints on the island, Crusader and Rags attempt to track the source. They find a table set with delicious foods, which turns out to be a trap. The pals are caged. Crusader and Rags are surprised to see their captor is Minnie, a Merbunny. She's a female rabbit mermaid. According to Alex Anderson, Grim Natwick, an illustrator on this adventure, came up with the Merbunny.

Minnie learns that Crusader and Rags came to help, thus she sets them free. She informs them about the pirates. Yes, they are real.

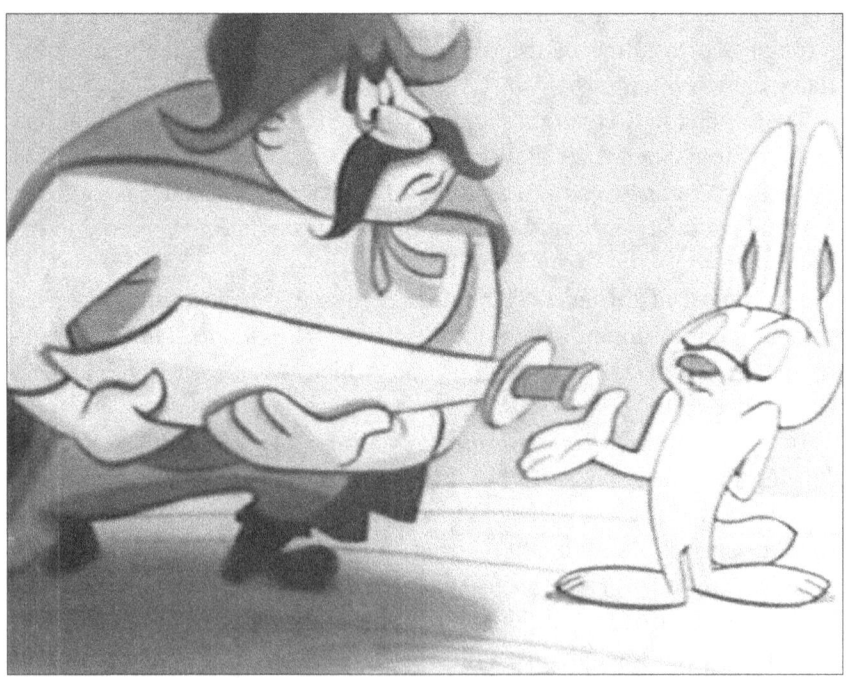

Crusader Rabbit meets Black Bilge in *Crusader Rabbit vs. the Pirates*.

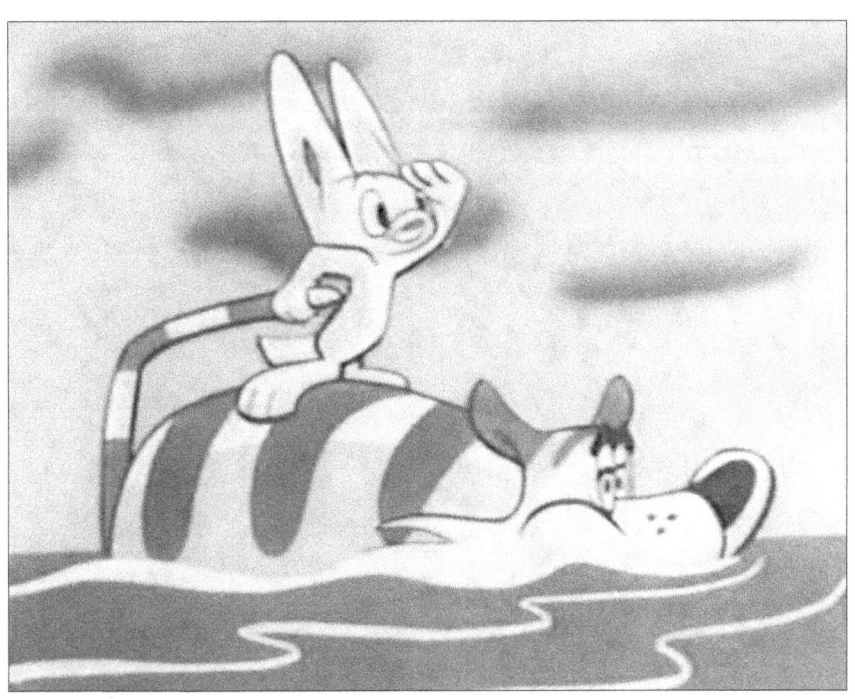

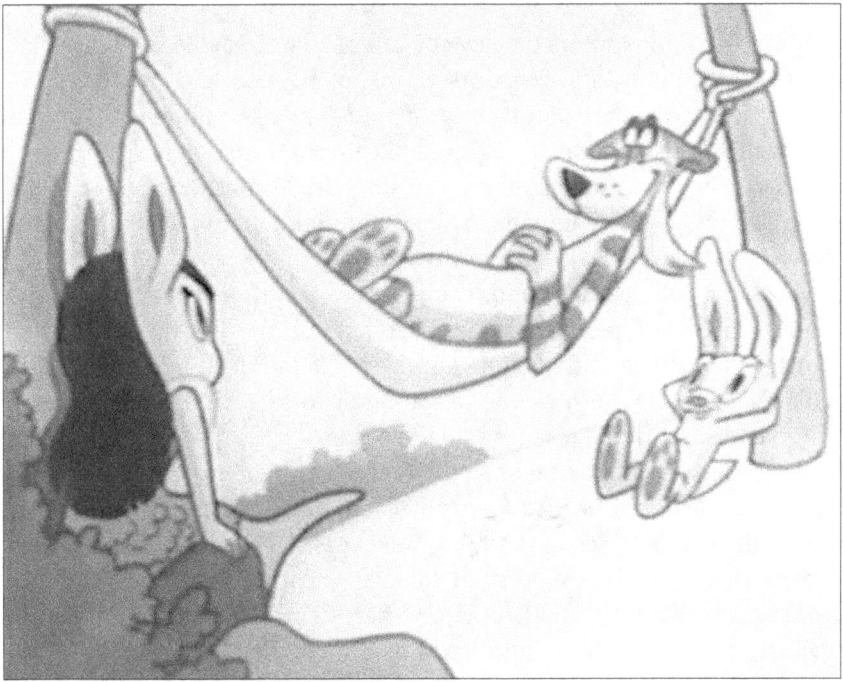

From *Crusader Rabbit vs. the Pirates*. Top, Crusader Rabbit uses Rags as a raft and navigates a course for Dunkin Island. Above, He and Rags meet Minnie, the Merbunny.

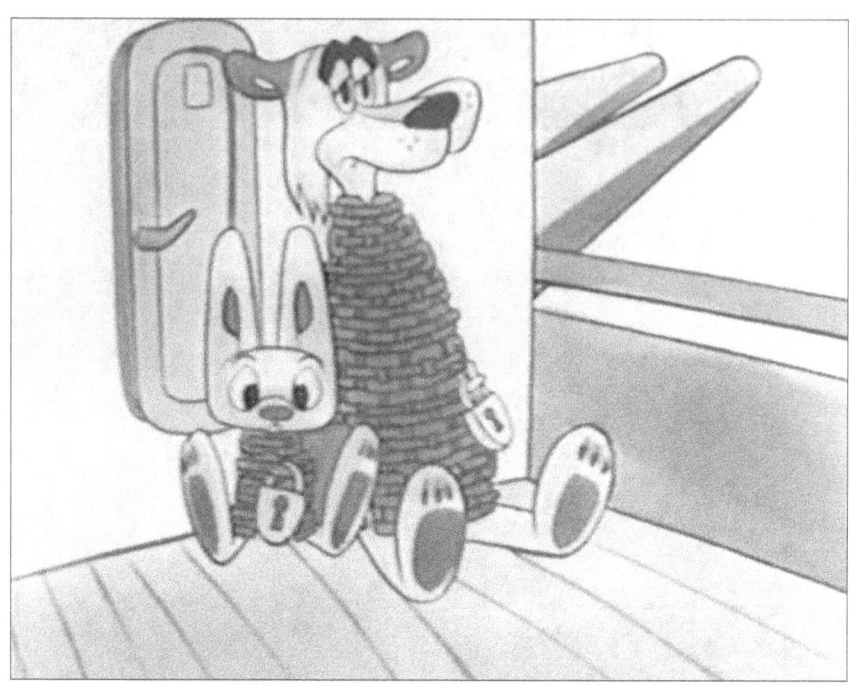

Crusader and Rags are held captive by Black Bilge in *Crusader Rabbit vs. the Pirates.*

Amusing things are on display at Dunkin Island, such as bananas that come with zippers, and coconuts with spigots. Also, the trap the Merbunny set for the hare and tiger is an amusing series of items that upon interacting present a Rube Goldberg-like mousetrap.

Black Blige the Pirate appears and snatches Minnie, taking her to his ship as a prisoner. He intends to make stew out of her to feed his hungry crew. Bilge has a sidekick, a mouthy parrot.

Crusader inflates Rags and, using him as a raft, catches up with the pirate ship, boarding her at night. Searching below deck they encounter danger, like sticks of dynamite. On deck, they find Minnie caged. Disguised as ship funnels, the heroes attempt to free Minnie. Buccaneers intervene, but Minnie escapes into the ocean.

Crusader and Rags challenge the crew, then Black Bilge, but are defeated. Crusader is next in line to become dinner. Bilge then spots an ocean liner and moves in to plunder the vessel. The small pirate ship is no match and sustains significant damage when the liner rams her.

Crusader escapes his dilemma and hides out aboard the pirate ship, evading the Buccaneers. Rags is trapped down below in a hold, unnoticed. Meanwhile, Black Bilge plots to hit New York City to steal all the silverware.

Crusader accidentally ends up inside of a bottle and winds up in the ocean. He uses his protruding feet as propellers to chase the pirate ship to shore to warn citizens of Bilge's plot.

After ending up placed among hundreds of other bottles in a wine cellar, the situation for Crusader seems dire. Black Bilge pulls into port and reconnects with a partner, the Professor, who is an octopus. The Professor, having nine arms, is the world's greatest pickpocket.

The Professor goes into the city and quickly snatches up silverware.

Crusader is taken out of the wine cellar and ends up beside the Admiral, where the hare manages to break the bottle. Free, Crusader alerts the Admiral of the thievery. The commander agrees to join the mission, but instead of being heralded as a crime-stopper, the rabbit is accused of being the criminal.

As bags of silver quickly fill up the pirate ship, Crusader, a fugitive from justice, flees. He acquires a raft with a motor and heads after Black Bilge, who has left the port. On Crusader's heels is the Admiral and a flotilla of warships in pursuit.

Crusader arrives at Dunkin Island, where Blige, the Professor, and the Buccaneers are busily burying the treasure.

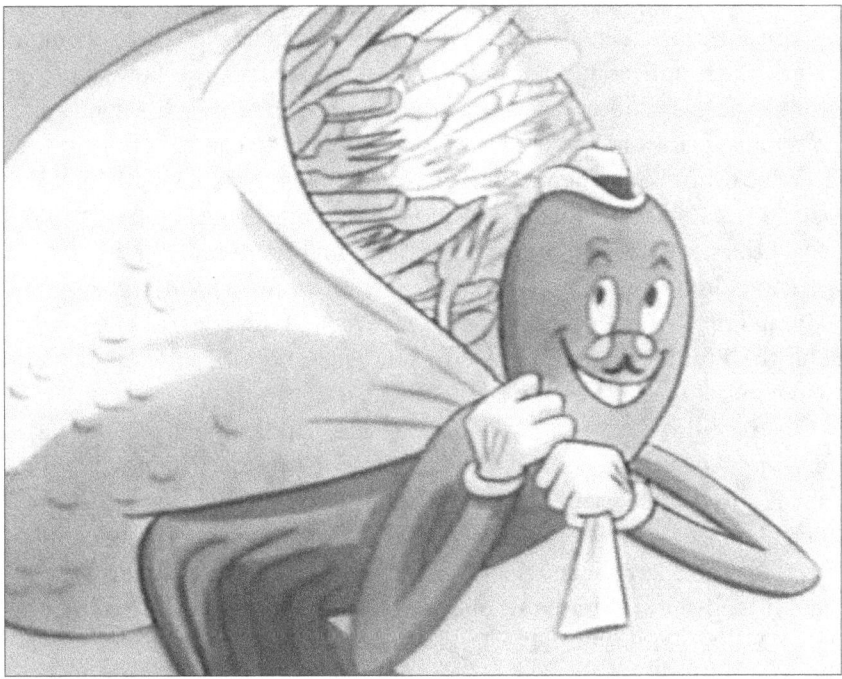

The Professor, a nine-legged octopus, stealing silverware in a scene from *Crusader Rabbit vs. the Pirates.*

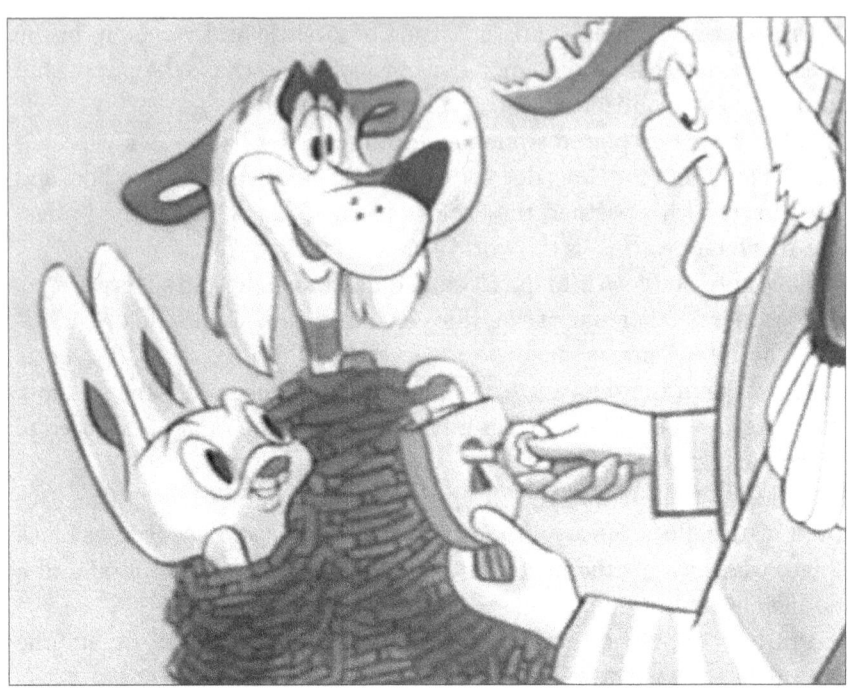

The Admiral, frees Crusader Rabbit and Rags in a scene from *Crusader Rabbit vs. the Pirates.*

Crusader swims beneath the pirate ship and pulls the plug, sinking it. Black Bilge notices his vessel is gone. Rags escapes the bowels of the sunken ship and reunites with Crusader. The rabbit uses his buddy as a raft to navigate and make their way to the island to confront the pirates.

Bilge captures the heroes and places them in a cooking kettle. But the island trembles, and sinks back into the sea. Bilge gives up trying to recover the treasure, and the hare and tiger safely float away in the pot.

The Admiral and his armada arrive. Crusader is vindicated when Minnie and her Merbunny friends recover the silverware. The pirates and the Professor are apprehended and sentenced to hard labor. Crusader and Rags, once again, are heralded as heroes.

In the third *Crusader Rabbit* adventure, Dudley Nightshade makes his series debut. The villain became Crusader's primary nemesis. Nightshade used the pseudonyms Whetstone Whiplash, and Ill-Regard Beauregard, on occasion. He operated with an oafish accomplice, Bilious Greene. Nightshade appeared in four adventures in the first series, and five adventures in the second series, which were filmed in color.

Crusader Rabbit and The Rajah of Rinsewater (20 Chapters). Everything was peaceful between man and beast in Rinsewater, India, before the Raja suddenly started trapping tigers and stealing their stripes to make India ink. The endangered tigers summon their cousin, Rags, and his partner, Crusader Rabbit, to find a solution. They discover the prime minister, Ali Oxenfree, a charitable, kindly leader, has appointed smooth-talking Dudley Nightshade to manage things. The con-man also is positioned to rob the province of all its treasure. Crusader and Rags sneak into the royal palace and kidnap the Raja in order to convince him Nightshade is mistreating his subjects and causing discord in the kingdom. The heroes even sew the Raja into a tiger costume so he can experience first-hand how the creatures are treated.

The first series of the *Crusader Rabbit* cartoon included seven more adventures. The episode titles and descriptions follow.

Crusader Rabbit and The Schmohawk Indians (15 Chapters). A tribe of fierce Indians, known as the Schmohawk, have been reduced to a bunch of wimps. They attempt to capture and consume Rags to gain his tiger strength and restore their pride. Crusader talks them out of it, recommending they pretend to go on the warpath to gain newspaper coverage and regain respect. But the public thinks it is real. The President of the United States dispatches the U.S. Army, commanded by General Horsewhip, to put down the uprising. Turning cowardly again, the Indians flee to the desert. There they meet Babyface Barracuda, former Public Enemy number one. Babyface gets the idea, with assistance from his gang, to rob area banks and pin it on the tribe. General Horsewhip captures Crusader and Rags, but they escape and free the Schmohawks who have been locked up in jail. Crusader and Rags then bring Babyface Barracuda and his mob to justice.

Crusader Rabbit and The Great Horse Mystery (20 Chapters). Andiron, the Fire Horse, summons Crusader and Rags to Oatville, Kentucky to investigate the disappearance of steeds. Oatville is the location of two industries, Potter's Paste and Glub's Glue. Kindly Peter Potter boasts his company produces the best adhesive, but evil Gaston Glub has something better. It's super glue. Crusader discovers the secret ingredient to Glub's paste is horse hooves. Glub and his gang accuse Potter, Crusader, and Rags of being the horse thieves. Crusader and Rags confront the challenge to clear their names, and Potter's. It's the only way to stop Glub from gaining a sizable government contract for his new, sticky invention.

Crusader Rabbit and The Circus (10 Chapters). Crusader and Rags pay a visit to the tiger's childhood home, the traveling circus of Colonel E. Pluribus Truepenny. But the once thriving and happy entertainment enterprise is on the skids, and Truepenny is nowhere to be found. His will, left behind, indicates he bestowed his circus business to twisted ringmaster, Whetstone Whiplash, and his sidekick, strongman Achilles the Heel. Whiplash captures and cages Rags, explaining he has merely recovered circus property. The heroic hare engages in a crusade to find Truepenny, and rescue the traveling show from Whetstone's possession.

Crusader Rabbit in The Tenth Century (30 Chapters). Crusader Rabbit and Rags travel back in time to Bedlam Castle in old England, courtesy of a court magician's spell. There, the hare and tiger discover the Blaggard brothers, Blackheart, Brimstone, and Bigot, are terrorizing the once peaceful countryside. The brothers are demanding the hand of Sir Chester Chillblain's gorgeous daughter, Mary Anne, in marriage. Crusader and Rags stuff themselves into one suit of armor, to win a tournament, defeating the Blaggards, and resolving the issue. But the brothers won't accept defeat, and kidnap Mary Anne and lock her up in a cell in their castle, which is guarded by a two-headed dragon, Arson, and Sterno. The heroes bypass the creature and sneak into Blaggard castle, freeing the damsel in distress. They also release the dragon by showing him their contract to work for the brothers is a recipe for gooseberry tarts. The troupe returns to Bedlam castle, with the Blaggard bunch in pursuit. The dragon helps defeat the scoundrels, and peace returns to Bedlam.

Crusader Rabbit and The Mad Hollywood Scientist (15 Chapters). Professor Belfrey Q. Batts is a marvelous inventor, but his other interest has proven to be a flop. His desire to become a star actor. Thus, he creates a gloom juice that can turn Hollywood actors ugly to level out the hiring playing field. He intends to use it out of revenge. Crusader and Rags confront Batts, attempting to persuade him to reverse his intent. But he seizes Rags and uses a machine to switch his brain with that of his assistant, Vernon, the vulture. Later Crusader and Vernon, with Rag's mind, break into the laboratory and administer Batts some of the gloom juice extract, which is a happiness potion. Batts, now reformed, joins the pair to try to stop Rags (with Vernon's brain) before he can spread the gloom juice, rendering all of Hollywood ugly. It's also a race against the clock to capture Rags and switch his brain back to Vernon before a fire destroys the machine that achieved the transformation.

Crusader Rabbit in The Leprechauns (25 Chapters). Crusader and Rags have new neighbors in their hometown of Galahad Glen: Leprechauns. They seem unthreatening, but their pots of gold attract fortune hunters, who ransack residents' homes looking for the valuable metal. Crusader investigates and discovers a greedy giant, Finn McCool XIII, had driven the Leprechauns out of their native land of Ireland. Thus, Crusader, Rags, Garfield Groundhog and chief Leprechaun Pat Finnegan travel there to rid the village of the Giant, so the transplanted elves can return. When they attempt to confront the beast at his cave, they discover no one has ever seen Finn McCool. However, they all know his secretary, Dudley Nightshade. Crusader suspects a ruse but has to prove Nightshade made up the Giant to acquire the land and the gold, as well.

Crusader Rabbit in The Showboat (25 Chapters). When Captain Huckleberry's floating entertainment business if figuratively sinking, Crusader, Rags, and Garfield Groundhog arrive to help. Huckleberry's old-time Mississippi river showboat, the Levee Belle, has been terrorized by the ghost of the Headless Oarsman, driving patrons way. If he doesn't raise money fast, Huckleberry will lose his mortgaged vessel. In short order, Crusader and his pals discover Whetstone Whiplash and his sidekick, Achilles the Heel, is behind the illusion. The dastardly cohorts, disguised as Sternwheel Jackson and Rhatt Butler, own the neighboring gambling boat, the Jezebel. Can Crusader and his pals expose the villains, raise money for the Captain, and prove Whiplash and Heel are also the culprits who robbed the Ripple town bank?

The entire *Crusader Rabbit* series received excellent reviews in trade magazines, with many stations reporting positive results. It has broadcast on over 200 stations, nationwide. The only criticism that surfaced was that the humor in the series was too geared for adults.

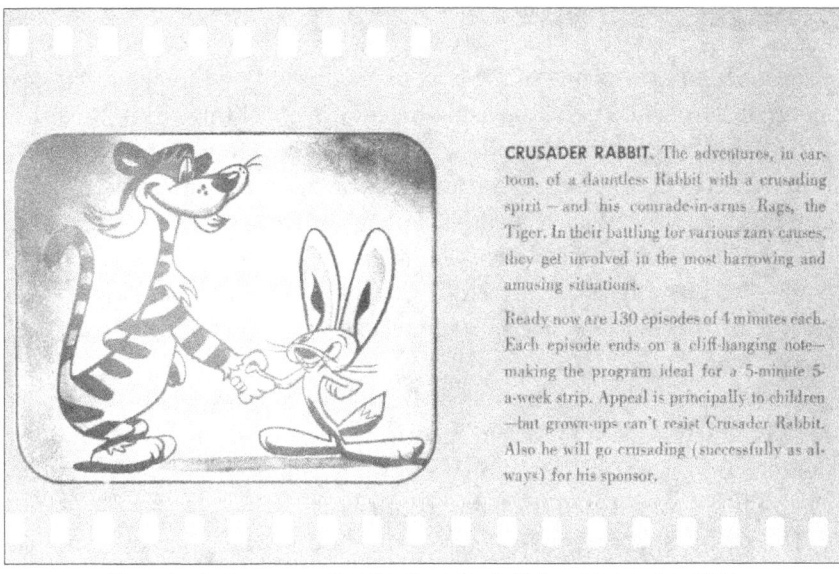

CRUSADER RABBIT. The adventures, in cartoon, of a dauntless Rabbit with a crusading spirit — and his comrade-in-arms Rags, the Tiger. In their battling for various zany causes, they get involved in the most harrowing and amusing situations.

Ready now are 130 episodes of 4 minutes each. Each episode ends on a cliff-hanging note—making the program ideal for a 5-minute 5-a-week strip. Appeal is principally to children —but grown-ups can't resist Crusader Rabbit. Also he will go crusading (successfully as always) for his sponsor.

Magazine feature promoting the *Crusader Rabbit* cartoon series, 1950.

Alex Anderson later commented, answering the critics, that he and Ward "thought kids were smarter than they got credit for."

But the gig was up. Funding was cut off in 1951. The final episodes were completed, and Television Arts Productions, Inc., essentially suspended operations, let its staff go, and closed its doors.

Alex Anderson found employment at the advertising agency Guild, Bascom and Bonfigli. Jay Ward went back into real estate.

Then, in 1953, disaster struck. Jerry Fairbanks Productions Inc. declared bankruptcy.

Alex Anderson and Jay Ward became aware something fishy was going on with the business side of *Crusader Rabbit* in early 1953, when they began reading stories in trade publications that NBC had taken Jerry Fairbanks to court.

They also learned that Consolidated Television Sales was selling the *Crusader Rabbit* series as part of a "pre-tested catalogue" of nine properties it had acquired.

"NBC did not name TAP as a defendant in its suit against Fairbanks, the complaint states," *Broadcasting* magazine reported. "The only knowledge the Berkeley firm [TAP] had of the network's obtaining the decree of foreclosure was from news stories."

The February 2, 1953 issue of *Broadcasting* reported NBC had filed a lawsuit on January 27. Fairbanks, who had borrowed $175,000 from the network, had paid only three $8,000 monthly payments before breaching the contract. Fairbanks had agreed to make 20 such installments.

Broadcasting was one of the first magazines to outline the arrangement with Consolidated Television Sales with its March 16, 1953 issue. Called the "Station-Starter Plan," Consolidated offered the *Crusader Rabbit* series in a package that included such other previously broadcast series as *Front Page Detective*, *Public Prosecutor*, *TV Closeups* and *Going Places with Uncle George*. All of the shows were Jerry Fairbanks Productions seized by NBC. Consolidated was created solely to resell Fairbank's productions for the recovery of money the network had lost on loans.

Broadcasting magazine reported on June 1, 1953, that Television Arts Productions, Inc. was engaged in a lawsuit seeking a temporary injunction against NBC, to stop them from selling the seized *Crusader Rabbit* films confiscated from Jerry Fairbanks.

The report stated that NBC had struck a deal with Fairbanks under which "it acquired title to the series," but in February 1952 "sold the

34

property back to him for $175,00 chattel mortgage."

After Fairbanks defaulted on payments, NBC won the legal right to seize all 195 *Crusader Rabbit* films.

The case went to court on October 19, but several days into the trial Anderson and Ward stuck back, targeting several parties for money owed to them to see if anything would stick.

Broadcasting magazine reported on October 26, 1953, that Television Arts Productions, Inc. had filed a breach of contract suit in Los Angeles Superior Court the previous day against Jerry Fairbanks, NBC, and Consolidated. TAP was seeking $400,000 due them in profits from sales of the 195 episodes. Anderson and Ward never saw a penny from the action, but the legal wrangling went on for some time.

During this period, Jay Ward was encouraged by longtime friends Leonard Key and Mike Lah to revive *Crusader Rabbit*. Ward contacted Alex Anderson about the prospect, but his former partner had happily settled into a more steady work as the creative director at the ad agency. Anderson declined to join in, but agreed to contribute some writing.

William Hanna partnered with Lah, resulting in the fledgling animation studio Shield Productions. The company was expressly established to produce an new *Crusader Rabbit* series in color. The studio brought in designers Don McNamara, Don Driscoll, and many of the old MGM animators. Lah's ambitious pitch to interested parties was for 195 new chapters. Lucille Bliss was back as Crusader, with Daws Butler as Rags. But only 11 episodes were completed before the project came to a halt.

Enter Shull Bonsall. He had purchased Consolidated Television Sales in February 1954, when it ceased operations. The transaction made him the owner of all 195 *Crusader Rabbit* film shorts.

In the summer of 1955, Bonsall purchased Creston Studios/TV Spots, a leading producer of animated television commercials. Thus, Bonsall was perfectly poised to make TV cartoons.

Why not be the next Paul Terry?

Bonsall had already made money on *Crusader Rabbit* since purchasing Consolidated Television Sales, placing the original series back into syndication. Former CTS, distributor George Bagnall and Associates, were in charge recycling the *Crusader* series. And Bonsall did so without any legal obligation to pay Alex Anderson or Jay Ward royalties.

Shull Bonsall was primarily an industry vulture, liquidator, and an opportunist. He hunted for cheap acquisitions. Controlling the messaging, Bonsall claimed he "rescued" failing media operations by taking them under his wing and "reorganizing" them. Translated, he bought

35

controlling interest and made money on the misfortune of others.

Bonsall entertained the notion of doing what Anderson, Ward, and Shield Productions were already engaged in—the production of an all-new, color *Crusader Rabbit* cartoon series.

Thus, Bonsall challenged the claim of who legally owned the Crusader Rabbit character and who had the right to produce a new TV series. The issue dragged Anderson and Ward, already weary and financially drained, back into court.

Television Arts Productions company had already lost a fortune due to Fairbanks' collapse. Now Fairbanks was working for Bonsall and making movies. TAP had no money coming in, just going out.

Television Arts Productions asserted in court that *Crusader Rabbit* belonged to them and NBC, and Jerry Fairbanks Productions, Inc. had no claim to ownership. The chain of sales involved ownership of the films only, not the character.

Anderson and Ward informed Bonsall if he wanted the copyright to *Crusader Rabbit*, he'd have to buy Television Arts Productions, Inc. Since the business had essentially been closed after turning out the final set of *Crusader Rabbit* chapters in 1951, Bonsall would be buying the name, and its properties, rather than a functioning studio.

Before Bonsall purchased TAP, he wanted to clear the company of any debt. Anderson informed him the corporation still owed him about $790,

FAIRBANKS PLANS TO RE-ENTER TV

PIONEER television producer Jerry Fairbanks, who withdrew from the syndication field about the time of the FCC tv freeze several years ago, announced last week he plans to re-enter the tv field with production of programs and commercial spots. Shull Bonsall, Hollywood financier, has purchased part interest in Jerry Fairbanks Productions and will be active in management of the firm, it was reported. The Fairbanks firm also will begin production of theatrical feature films for release through the major studios, but the product may also be released to tv.

Mr. Bonsall has purchased controlling interest in Tv Spots Inc., Hollywood producer of animated commercials, which will continue to operate separately from the Fairbanks firm although services will be integrated and made available to all clients.

Mr. Fairbanks continues as president of his own film company with Mr. Bonsall becoming executive vice president and treasurer. Mr. Bonsall will be in charge of all business and financial activities, it was explained, with Mr. Fairbanks supervising production and creative work.

Jerry Fairbanks Productions is expanding its physical facilities and will have completed construction of a large modern studio in downtown Hollywood within the next 60 days, Mr. Fairbanks said. Pilot films for prospective new tv half-hour shows are in preparation. It is hoped to sell them for network first-run with subsequent local syndication, he explained.

Affiliation of Messrs. Fairbanks and Bonsall began several years ago when Mr. Bonsall purchased various Fairbanks' properties for open-end tv release.

Broadcasting magazine, April 23, 1956.

and suggested if he was allowed to keep the unsold characters he had created while at TAP, and some camera equipment, the issue would be settled. Bonsall agreed.

Little could Bonsall have known that among the unsold character properties were the copyrights to *Rocky the Flying Squirrel*, *Bullwinkle the Moose*, and *Dudley Do-Right*. Anderson also kept an unsold series pilot film, *The Frostbite Falls Review*, which featured the first animated appearance of Rocky and Bullwinkle.

Then Anderson sold 50% of the character rights to Jay Ward for around $390. Anderson thought it was only fair, as the characters were created for the purpose of their television partnership venture.

Bonsall completed the purchase of Television Arts Productions, Inc. in May 1956, paying Alex Anderson and Jay Ward the sum of $50,000.

As a result, Shield Productions shelved the 11 completed *Crusader Rabbit* cartoons they had produced. None were publically released.

William Hanna rejoined his pal Joseph Barbera to establish their own animation studio, with the talents at Shield finding employment there.

Perhaps the only good thing to emerge from the *Crusader Rabbit* fiasco with Shull Bonsall was it resulted in the establishment of Hanna Barbera Studios. The partners, who had known each other since 1939 while working for MGM, went on to establish the gold standard for television animation, introducing the most successful cartoon characters and series of all time.

The "unsold properties" Anderson saved, *Rocky*, *Bullwinkle*, and the original concept for *Dudley Do-Right*, would be used to launch Jay Ward Studios a short time later.

Anderson moved up the scale during his 17 years at Guild, Bascom and Bonfigli, eventually becoming the ad agency's president.

Crusader Rabbit resurfaced as a survivor of the court drama and would be up and hopping for round two of his television adventures. Shull Bonsall's TV Spots would produce the new series, without any input from Anderson or Ward. A few former TAP employees and talents were hired by TV Spots and participated in the new color series.

So, while Anderson and Ward were not back, some of their former employees were, which provided some continuity. The general public welcomed the announced return of the series, and television stations expressed enthusiasm, signing up in record numbers.

But could Crusader Rabbit and Ragland T. Tiger again see victory after surviving a hostile takeover?

Find out in our next chapter.

The Cast of Characters

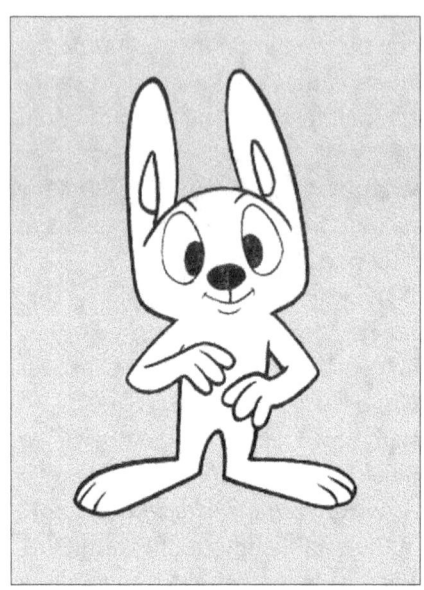

Crusader Rabbit
Our hero.

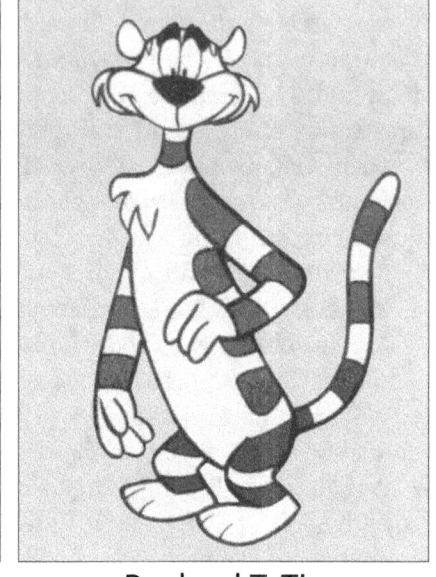

Ragland T. Tiger
Crusader's best friend.

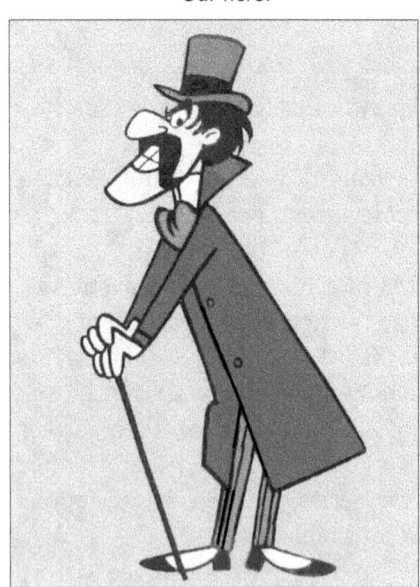

Dudley Nightshade
Crusader's #1 enemy.

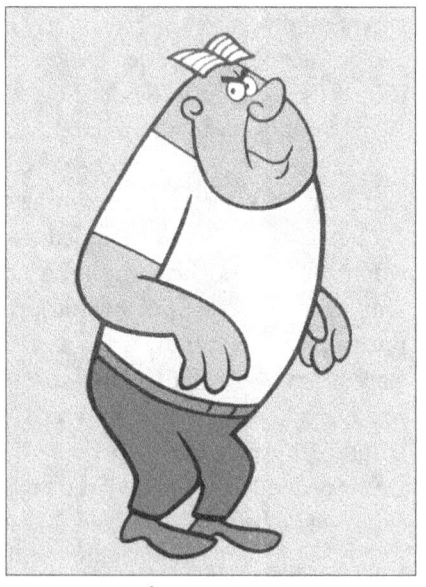

Bilious Greene
Dudley Nightshade's nasty assistant.

The Cast of Characters

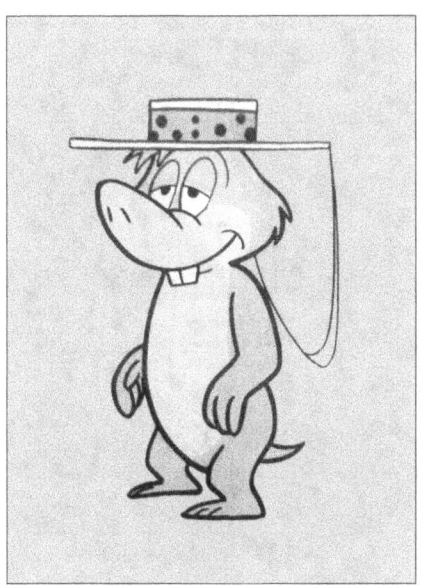

Garfield Groundhog
Friend of Crusader and Rags.

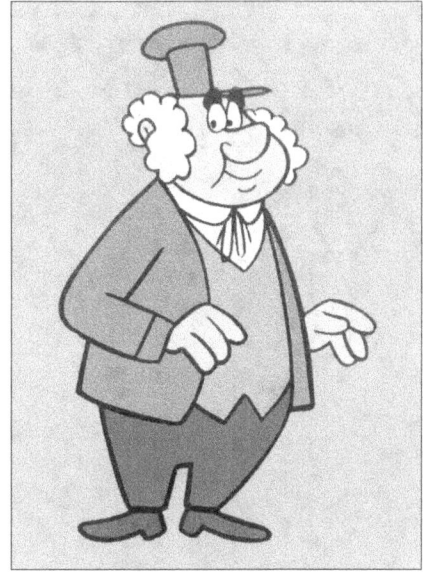

Captain Huckleberry
Riverboat operator and friend.

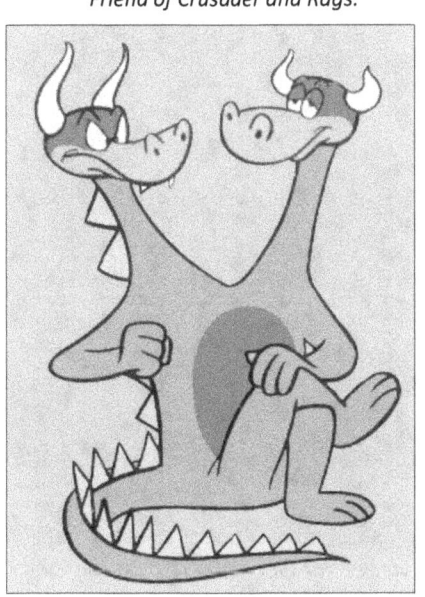

Arson and Sterno
The two-headed dragon.

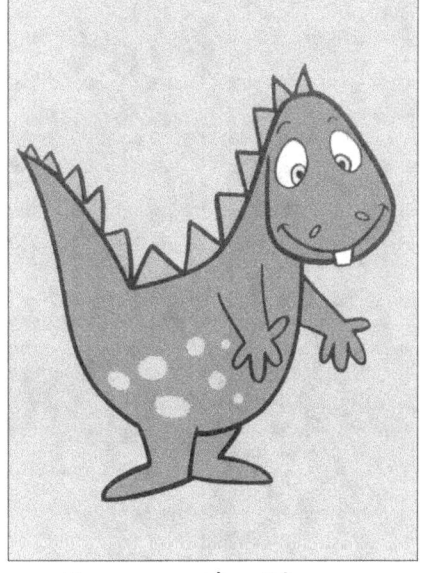

Seymour the Dinosaur
A prehistoric toddler friend.

The Cast of Characters

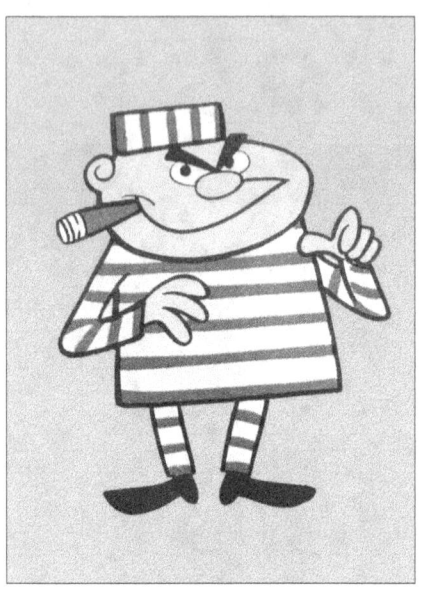

Sam Quentin
Criminal and escaped prisoner.

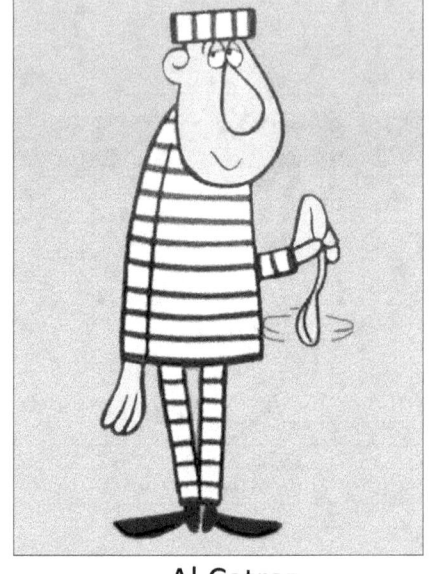

Al Catraz
Quentin's crooked sidekick.

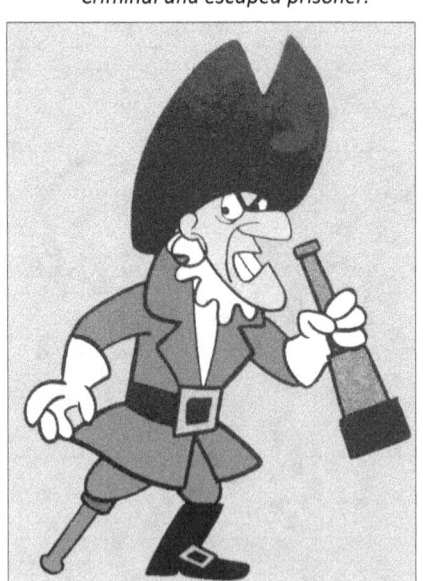

Captain Jolly Roger
Pirate and navigation pain.

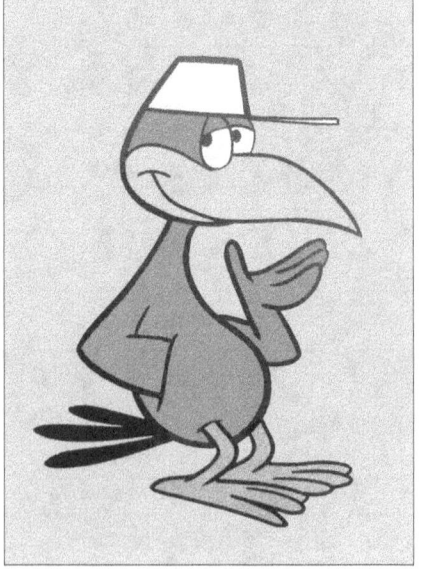

S. Crow
A bit flighty, at best.

CHAPTER FOUR

The Return of Crusader Rabbit

Shull Bonsall was born June 30, 1917, in Los Angeles, California. He was the son of Howard and Catherine Bonsall. His first name came from his mother's last name, Catherine Shull. His father was one of Los Angeles' first successful businessmen, working as a railroad president, real estate executive, and mortgage and loan officer.

Growing up, Shull Bonsall lived in a spacious mansion in Beverly Hills. He had one sibling, a brother, nearly three years older, named Curtis, who became an attorney.

Bonsall's first significant buy on his pathway to television production was the acquisition of TV Spots Inc. in the summer of 1955. He retained the president of TV Spots, Robert Wickersham, to continue operating the company, providing continuity.

But Bonsall wasn't prone to conduct business as usual. Thus, he quickly ran into trouble with the National Labor Relations Board. As a result, the Screen Cartoonists Guild targeted TV Spots, shutting the studio down on January 3, 1956.

"The Screen Cartoonists Guild [is] striking one company, TV Spots,

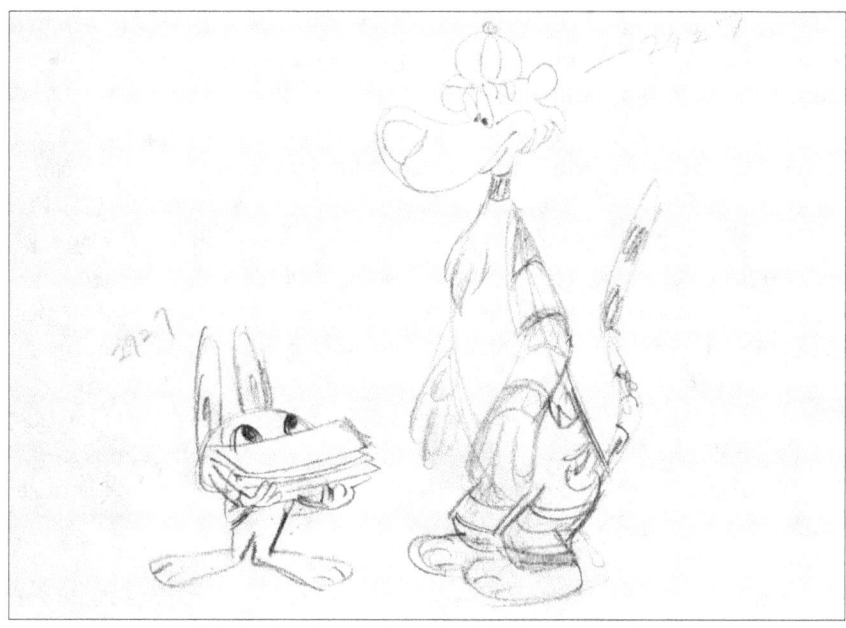

A sketch for the new *Crusader Rabbit* cartoon series.

41

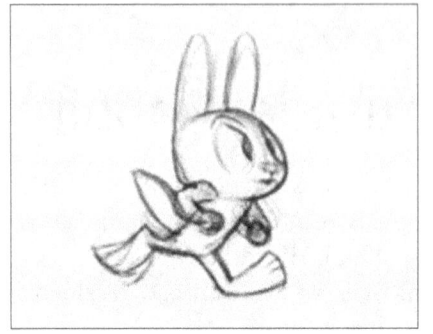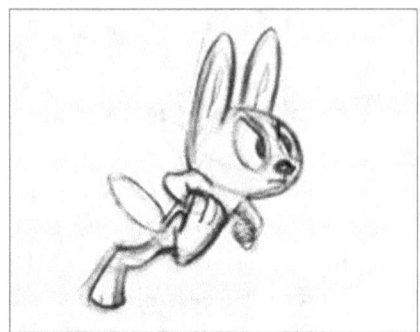
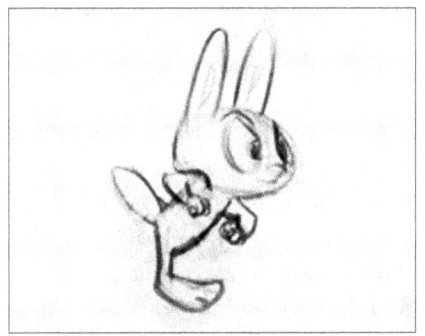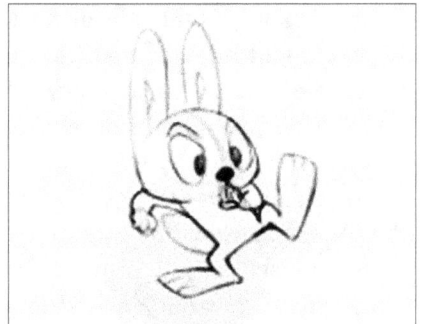

Sketches for the new *Crusader Rabbit* cartoon series.

and six others, promptly closing their doors to present a united front," *Billboard* reported on January 21st.

Roughly six months after purchasing TV Spots, it was closed for business. Its' employees, along with others in the industry, staged pickets outside of the locked studio doors.

"With the settlement of the recent labor dispute, all studios except TV Spots and Swift-Chaplin in this area will be resuming 100% operations as soon as possible," the Screen Cartoonists Guild announced in the February issue of *Business Screen Magazine*. "There will be no stoppages in getting your message to the telecasting public."

The SCG sought to raise the pay scale of animators from $160 per week to $185. But Bonsall wasn't budging and remained adamant, refusing to bargain.

"At press time the sole holdouts to signing [the SCG contract] included TV Spots Inc., which was the first target of the SCG's strike action," *Billboard* reported on February 18. "New wage minimums will raise animators from $160 per week to $185."

Billboard reported a proposal for commissions on work had been defeated. But animators and illustrators who were on strike or laid off would recover lost wages.

Bonsall eventually signed the SCG contract, but news of the dispute and how TV Spots had little regard for its employees, did major damage. Some of the talent returned to their jobs, but some didn't. Finding new animators and illustrators wasn't easy. Who would want to work there?

In a public relations move, Bonsall replaced Wickersham with Jerry Fairbanks as president of TV Spots in April.

Fairbanks had defaulted on his NBC loans, causing him to file bankruptcy, but the misfortune didn't hurt his reputation for inventive, quality production. He was still respected.

Working his way into the industry, Bonsall had a knack for dreaming up company names for operations he owned. Press releases issued often rattled off a series of entities connected to the marketing of his properties. In the case of *Crusader Rabbit*, it was no different.

Bonsall registered names for no less than half a dozen "companies" that were involved in marketing, licensing, and distributing the *Crusader Rabbit* character and series.

In 1956, Bonsall established Ramlen Associates as the company identified as the owner of Television Arts Productions, Inc. and exclusive owners of *Crusader Rabbit*. He had organized the company shortly after the May 1956 sale and appointed Dick Moses to head the operation.

By the fall of 1956, Ramlen Associates primarily became a department securing print and publication arrangements for *Crusader Rabbit*, such

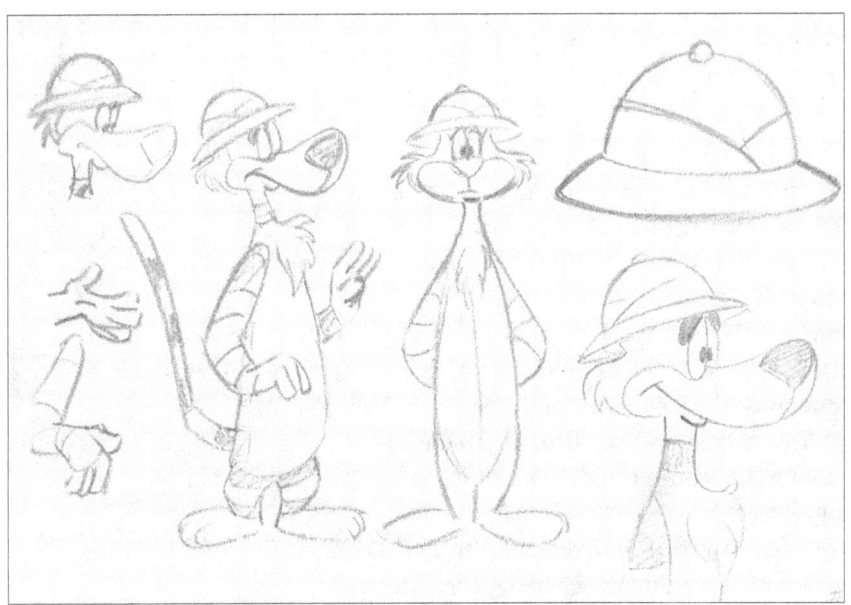

A sketch for the new *Crusader Rabbit* cartoon series.

43

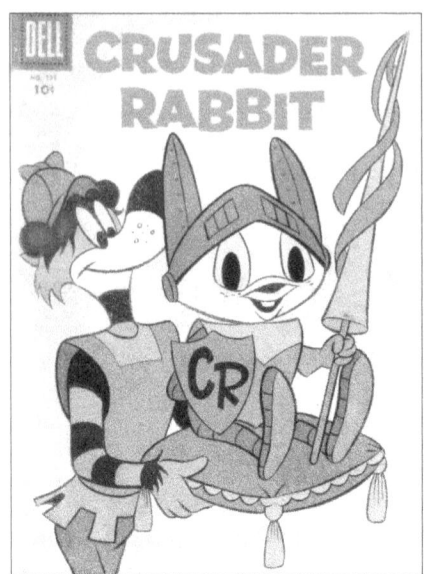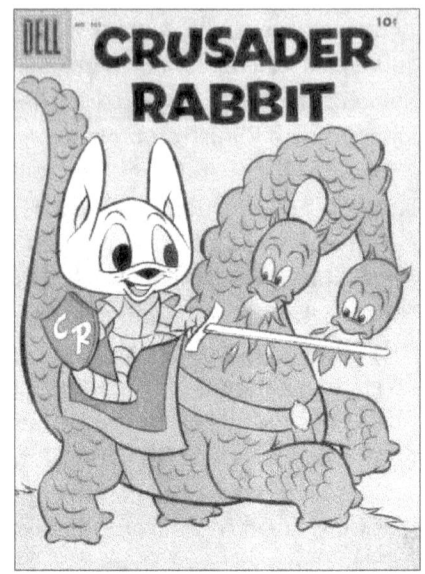

The two *Crusader Rabbit* comic books published by Dell, 1956 and 1957.

as coloring, activity and comic books.

Ramlen swung a deal with Dell Comics, which published two issues of *Crusader Rabbit*. The first Dell *Crusader Rabbit* appearance came in *Four Color* comics #735 in October 1956. A second issue came in June 1957, in *Four Color* #805.

Bonsall also set up Crusader Rabbit Sales Inc. to distribute the series. This company was in the same office as Ramlen. Initially, Bonsall kept Television Arts Productions, Inc. as the identifier of the *Crusader Rabbit* film series brand, while stating Ramlen owned all rights.

Ramlen being Bonsall, of course.

Billboard magazine announced in its' November 3rd issue that sales of the new Crusader Rabbit cartoon series were inching up to $1 million.

"The new *Crusader Rabbit* animated series has now been sold in over 40 markets, representing $800,000 in gross business," *Billboard* reported. "The property is now owned by Ramlen Associates, headed by Dick Moses, which bought the rights last May from Television Arts Productions, the originator of the cartoon character."

The article stated all of the business/sales was brought in by telephone. It also reported, "The series is due to make its air debut in January [1957]."

Billboard said on December 29 that Leonard Key had been installed as Ramlen president, replacing Dick Moses.

Key, an old friend of Jay Ward, had been one of the individuals that encouraged him to bring back *Crusader Rabbit* earlier, leading to the establishment of Shield Studios, which created 11 animated films for the proposed series before Bonsall put the kibosh on it and purchased TAP.

Now Key was working for Bonsall.

"The new *Crusader Rabbit* series has gone into full production and will make its air debut in February, at which time Television Arts Productions expects to be turning out five episodes a week," *Billboard* reported on December 29. "Leonard Key has been elected president of both Ramlen Inc., which owns the literary, production and merchandising rights, and Crusader Rabbit Sales Inc., which is distributing it."

Billboard reported that Key had sold the new *Crusader Rabbit* series to 53 markets thus far, 28 of which would be sponsored by members of the American Bakery Co-operative.

"He [Key] has also been merchandising the property quite vigorously, having licensed 46 items, including games and stuffed toys," *Billboard* added.

Billboard stated that one "unusual" part of the merchandising arrangement was that television stations buying the series would get a "20% cut of the royalties" on sales made in their markets.

Billboard also announced the new series would be titled *The New Adventures of Crusader Rabbit and Rags the Tiger*, a long unused title. "Key hopes to make 260 episodes," the magazine added.

Leonard Key had previously been the sales manager for Shamus Culhane Productions, Inc. That company produced animation and live action films for entertainment and commercial purposes.

Key's tenure at Ramlen ended in April 1957, when he took a job as an account executive for Economee TV. With his departure, the name Ramlen disappeared, also. The brand Television Arts Productions eventually became the merchandising entity of Bonsall's operations.

The truth of the matter was Bonsall's operation was raising capital on hype, merchandising, and redistribution of the original black and white series, playing on the anticipation of a new color series.

As an example, the Dell comic books featuring *Crusader* licensed by Bonsall saw publication way before the new series of films were available to TV stations.

Billboard reported on September 9, 1957, that the first completed films in the series could see broadcast by the end of that month.

"A new series of *Crusader Rabbit* cartoons are being put into production by Shull Bonsall and TV Spots," *Billboard* reported. "A total of 260 of the episodes will be turned out on 35mm color [film]."

45

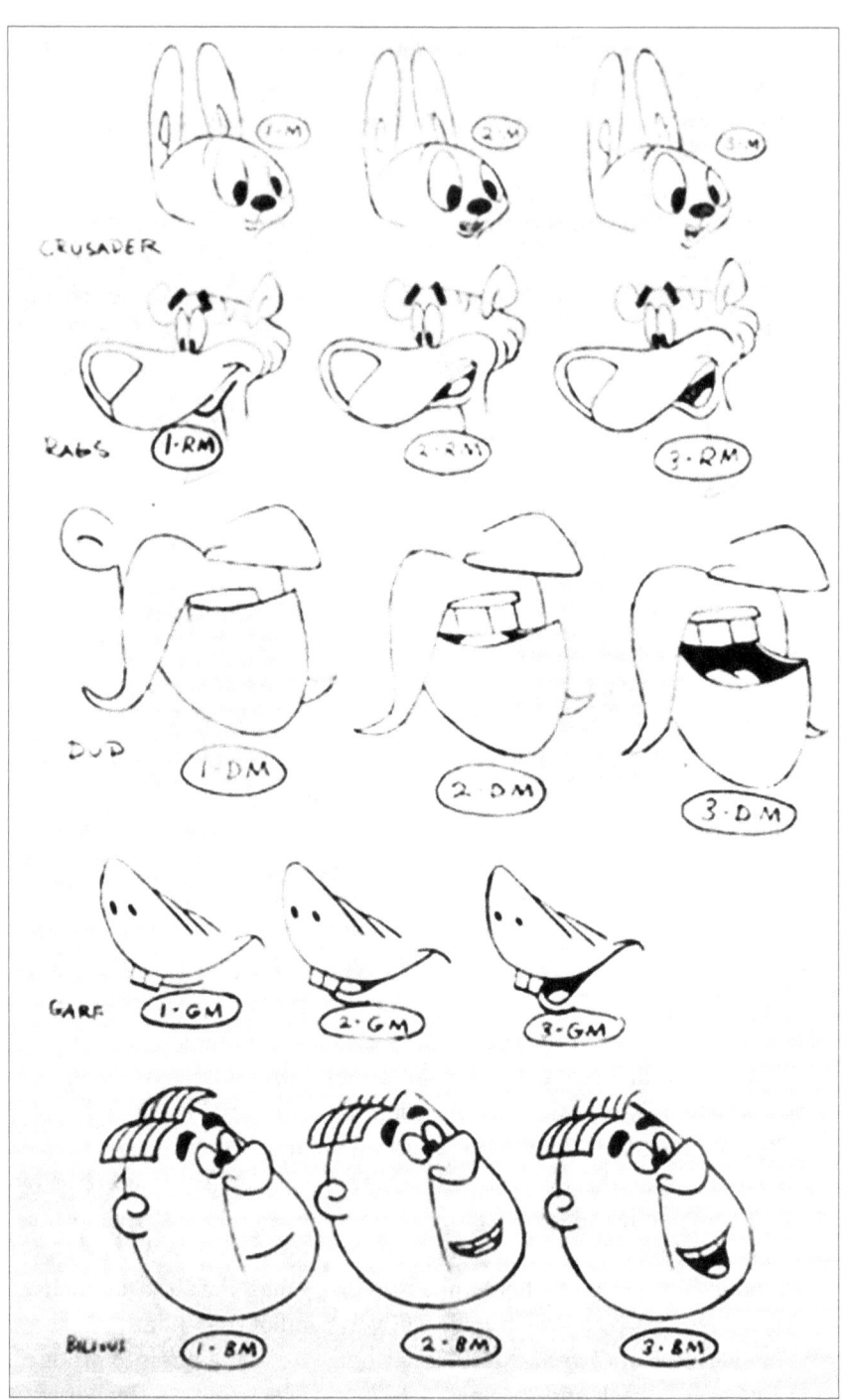

Left side of a second series *Crusader Rabbit* model sheet.

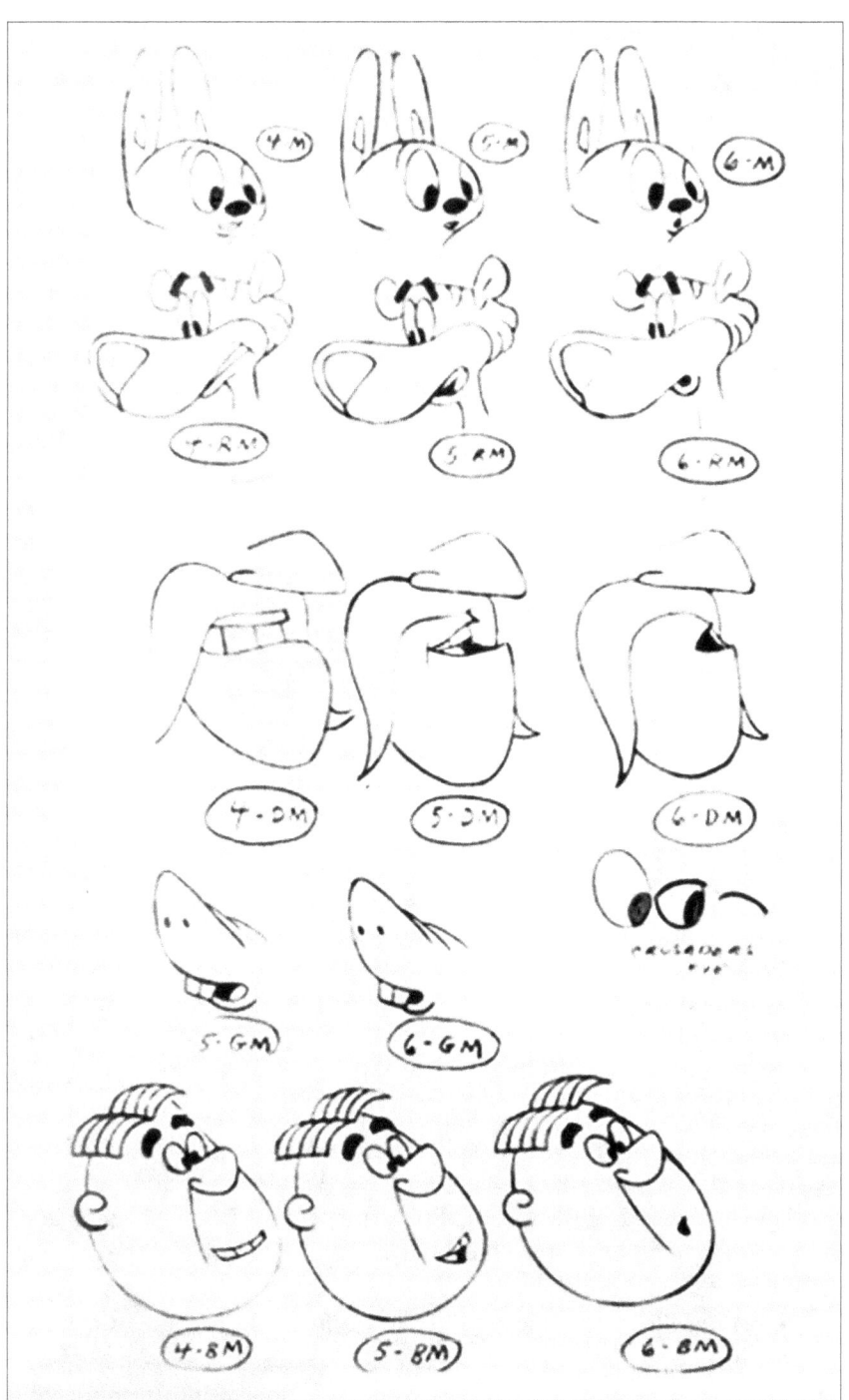

Right side of a second series *Crusader Rabbit* model sheet.

In the article, Bonsall stated the films would cost "about $3,500" per episode, or "$900,000 for 260 segments." The program was pitched as individual spots to feature within a local program, or put together in groups of 15 for a 30 minute *Crusader Rabbit* show.

"The first of the new films will be ready for showing the end of this month," *Billboard* said. "No distribution has been set so far."

Sponsor magazine reported the new series would be offered to agencies beginning October 29th.

But it didn't happen.

Pre-production for the new series of *Crusader Rabbit* actually began sometime in the summer of 1957. It took about a year for TV Spots to recover from the damage caused concerning the strike. But it was only later in the year that many of the talented folks that had worked on the original *Crusader Rabbit* series, along with other established animation professionals, agreed to work for TV Spots.

Only then did the push needed to make the series a reality take place. The planned 260 chapters, comprising 13 adventures, were actually placed into full production.

The producer of the new *Crusader Rabbit* series was Lee Orgel, who worked closely with director Sam Nicholson.

Orgel, who had previously worked as the producer of Jack and Chuck Luchsinger's *Cartoon TeleTales*, went on to form his own production company, Jomar Productions. There he developed and produced numerous shows including *The New Adventures of the Three Stooges*, and the *Abbott and Costello* cartoon series.

Nicholson went on to produce *King Leonardo and His Short Subjects* and *Galaxy High School*.

Bob Ganon served as production supervisor, with Dave Hoffman as the production planner.

Ganon and Hoffman subsequently both worked on *King Leonardo and His Short Subjects* and *Calvin and the Colonel*.

Three of the primary voices on the original series signed onto the new series. Returning were announcer, Roy Whaley, Vern Louden as Ragland T. Tiger, and Russ Coughlin as the voice of Dudley Nightshade, and a bunch of other nasty villains. Lucille Bliss, the voice of the original heroic hare, would not be back.

Shull Bonsall had contacted Bliss to perform the voice of Crusader Rabbit again, but she turned it down when he offered to pay her $5 per chapter, instead of union scale $35. Bliss got Bonsall into trouble with the Screen Actors Guild for this, who formed a picket line outside the TV

Spots studio.

It was another labor relations nightmare on public display that TV Spots didn't need. But, it didn't have anything to do with the SCG contract resolving the animator issue, so Bonsall remained defiant.

He responded by blackballing Bliss, and threatening anyone who might hire her. This included Hanna Barbera. Bonsall indicated he'd destroy the little, upstart animation company.

Eventually, Hanna Barbera and others did gainfully employ Bliss after the heat cooled off.

Actress GeGe Pearson was hired to play the new voice of Crusader Rabbit. Pearson was a veteran radio actress. She, like Bliss, went on to work as a voice artist for Hanna Barbera.

The writers on the new series included newcomers Chris Bob Hayward and Barbara Chain.

Bob Ganon commented on Hayward's writing ability in the November 1982 issue of *Comics Scene* magazine.

"Chris Hayward did a good job, but I've always felt he could never quite capture Alex Anderson's view of the characters," Bob Ganon said. "Nevertheless, he did a very credible job. The words were funny, but not quite as pure as Alex's. He was a great genius in that, I think."

Hayward subsequently worked as a writer for Jay Ward's *Rocky and Bullwinkle* series and co-created *The Munsters* TV show with Allan

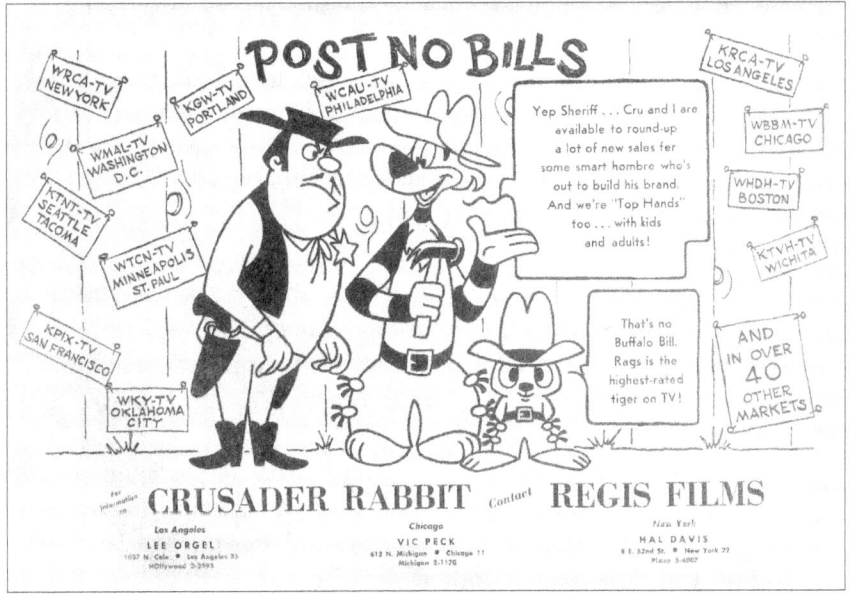

Advertisement for the new *Crusader Rabbit* series, distributed by Regis Films.

Burns. Burns had worked for Ward at the same time Hayward did. He was responsible for creating *Cap'n Crunch* and his crew for a series of animated cereal commercials, produced by Ward's studio.

Barbara Chain went on to become a writer for *The Famous Adventures of Mr. Magoo* series, and the *Rambo* cartoon, among others. Jack Miller, a writer on the first series, returned for the second. Miller had co-written the adventures *Circus* and *Tenth-Century* adventures.

Miller's first recognizable work as an animation writer came with the release of *Have You Got Any Castles*, in 1938, for Leon Schlesinger Studios. Subsequently, his resume increased, with work for *The New Three Stooges* and as a storyboard artist for animated Filmation's *Star Trek* series, 1973-74.

Miller commented on the second *Crusader Rabbit* series in the November 1982 issue of *Comics Scene*.

"Color TV was just coming in then," Jack Miller said. "We asked the boss if we could go around the corner to the bar and see the first episodes [on their color TV]. Well, the drunks in there were horrified that we wanted to see this cartoon. They wanted to watch baseball!"

Art Becker provided music for the series, but virtually all of it was "stock tunes." Ray Erlenborn and Gene Twambley were placed in charge of sound effects.

Returning animators and artists, who had worked on the first series, included Bob Bastian, Bob Bemiller, and John Sparey. Also returning was background artist Volney White.

New animators and illustrators to the series included Alex Ignatiev, Bob Matz, Reuben Timmins, Joseph Price, and Marv Woodward. Background artists included David Weidman, Eleanor Bogardus, and Rosemary O'Connor. In charge of ink and paint were Martha Buckley and Maggi Alcumbrac (Raymond). Ed Levitt was in charge of layouts.

Alex Ignatiev, who began his career working for Leon Schlesinger Studios in 1939, went on to work for Hanna Barbera, assigned to such series as *Jonny Quest*, *The Flintstones*, and *Scooby-Doo*.

Bob Matz went on to work for DePatie-Freleng Enterprises, and was a director on series such as *The Transformers*, *Muppet Babies* and a string of *Charlie Brown* specials.

Reuben Timmins went on to work on the cartoon series *Spider-Man*, *Star Trek*, and *Flash Gordon*. Marv Woodward, a former Disney animator, subsequently worked on *Mr. Magoo* and *Linus the Lionhearted*.

Ed Levitt began his career working for Disney on such films as *Snow White and the Seven Dwarfs*, *Fantasia,* and *Bambi*. Later he worked on a series of *Charlie Brown* animated specials.

Artists Weidman, Bogardus, and O'Connor subsequently accumulated impressive resumes in the animation world.

Julian E. Raymond and Ted Bemiller served as cameramen, with film editing by Charles McCann and Norman Vizents.

Ted Bemiller was the brother of Bob Bemiller. He subsequently worked on such animated features as *Hey There, It's Yogi Bear*, and Ralph Bakshi's *Heavy Traffic*. He also worked on several animated *Garfield* specials.

Billboard reported on February 10, 1958, that the new *Crusader Rabbit* series was in production and announced Bonsall had created Regis Films, a company that would distribute the series.

"A new *Crusader Rabbit* animated TV series, designed to appeal directly to adult as well as juvenile viewers, is being produced at the Hollywood studios of TV Spots Inc. and will be offered to stations and sponsors by Regis Films," *Billboard* reported. "Both companies are owned by California industrialist Shull Bonsall, a onetime associate of Jerry Fairbanks, from whom the rights to *Crusader Rabbit* were acquired."

Billboard reported the series was being filmed using 35mm Eastman color film, from which 16mm prints would be available in both color and black and white.

"Two units now are turning out 1,400 feet a week of completed animated cartoon film, said by Mr. Bonsall to be the highest output of any company in the country," *Billboard* reported.

Overseeing the effort was TV Spots vice president and general manager, Bill Bauman.

Sponsor magazine also announced the Regis Films plan in its February 22, 1958 issue.

Bonsall put the company brand name of Capitol Enterprises on the completed *Crusader Rabbit* film cartoons. It was more like a "capital" enterprise. The name established to cover all of Bonsall's *Crusader Rabbit* operations.

Sponsor magazine reported on March 8, 1958, that "a second animation unit has gone into full production" on the *Crusader Rabbit* color TV cartoon series and "a third unit would begin production this month."

By March 15 a third unit was on the job at TV Spots, bring the number of staffers to a total of 60 artists, scripters, and animators working on the series.

Billboard reported the pace was expected to yield, "an unprecedented total of 2,400 feet of complete animation, or six five–minute episodes, per week."

That spring enough episodes were in the can to physically begin getting the cartoon into the hands of broadcasters. One amusing piece of trivia is that Jay Ward's new animation effort made the news as *Crusader Rabbit* was officially ready to launch. And the news item mentioned *Crusader Rabbit*, as well.

Sponsor magazine reported on May 2, 1958, that General Mills would be sponsoring "an original cartoon series, *Rocky and His Friends*,

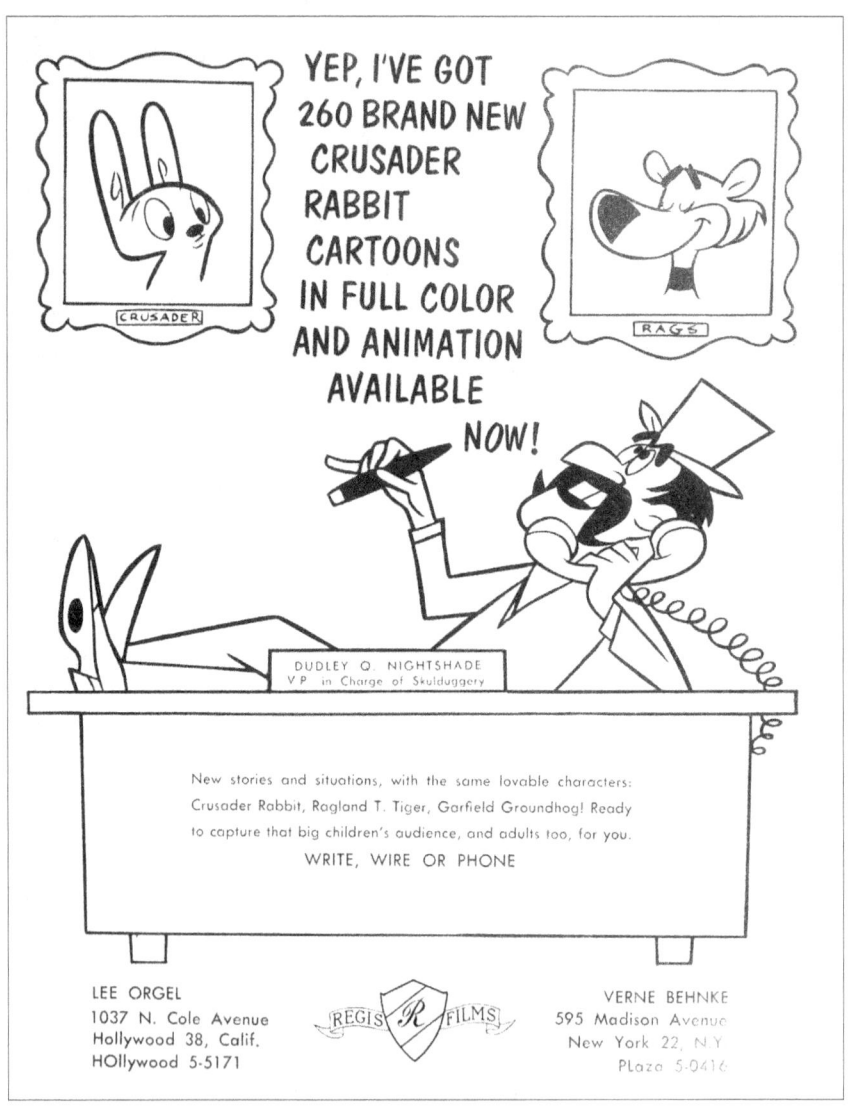

Advertisement for the new *Crusader Rabbit* series, distributed by Regis Films.

to be turned out by Producers Associates for Television, creators of *Crusader Rabbit*."

It was a friendly reminder that the character originated from Ward's previous studio, Television Arts Productions Inc.

The first actual sales and distribution of the new *Crusader Rabbit* series to stations was reported in *Broadcasting* magazine, on June 9.

Stations included: WBBM-TV in Chicago, WHDH-TV in Boston, WPIX-TV in San Francisco, WMAL-TV in Washington, and KGMB-TV of Honolulu, among others. The stations and many others buying the series package began broadcasting the new, color, *Crusader Rabbit* adventures in early summer.

Sponsor magazine reported months later, in its August 23 edition, that the new series had "accounted for $750,000 in sales" for distributor Regis Films.

Stations buying the series reported seeing profits immediately.

Broadcasting magazine announced on November 3, 1958, "If you were a young fan of *Crusader Rabbit*, the TV cartoon hero, you would no doubt be interested in these and other unusual premiums and retail toys."

The magazine listed several items, including a floating, plastic showboat and a paper puppet punch-out kit.

By then merchandising was in full swing, and the Bonsall property Television Arts Productions was officially shortened to TAP, and promoted as the "merchandisers of the *Crusader Rabbit* series and developers of toy products."

The 13 new adventures brought back Crusader Rabbit and Ragland T. Tiger, as well as their arch enemy, Dudley Nightshade, and sidekick, Bilious Greene. Shull Bonsall also edited full adventures together as one-hour films for theatrical release, but the format never caught on. The movies were test marketed in a few theaters with unenthusiastic results.

TV cartoons weren't designed to the quality standards of theatrical animated films. It was worth a shot, but exhibitors were not interested.

A list of episode titles with a story synopsis follows. Alternate titles also appear for movie editions.

Crusader Rabbit in The Great Uranium Hunt (20 episodes). *Mine Your Own Business* (one-hour movie format). Crusader and Rags arrive back home to the Galahad Glen train depot to discover a gambler named E. Z. Moony has foreclosed on the community. He opened a casino and won the town by cheating, which is how he plays the game. Crusader confronts the shyster, who demands $420,000 to repurchase it. Garfield

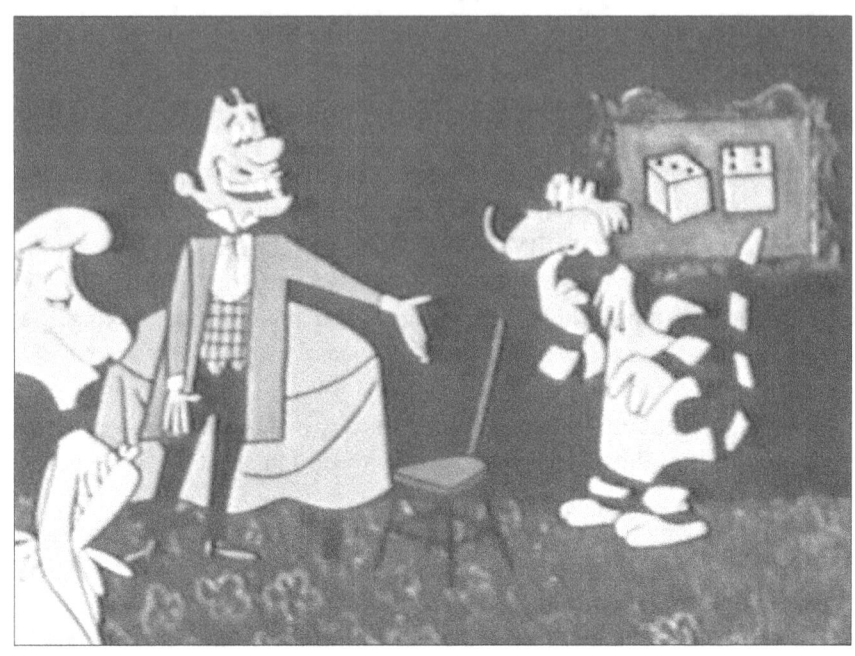

A scene from Crusader Rabbit in The Great Uranium Hunt.

Groundhog suggests Crusader Rabbit and Rags go prospecting for uranium. If they strike it rich, they can repurchase their town. Dudley Nightshade, along with Bilious Greene, arrive in town with their scheme. Dudley invests in Crusader's mining company, but the form Rags signs isn't granting a share. It's a phony life insurance policy, with Dudley as the beneficiary. The giant rock Dudley drops on Rags to snuff him out turns out to be a dinosaur egg. Thus, Seymour, the baby dino is hatched. The creature has such a lovely voice, Dudley and Bilious try to capture it to sell as an entertainment act for TV. Besides, Seymour thinks Rags and Crusader are his parents. Failing to acquire the creature, Nightshade convinces Moony to cancel the debt on Galahad Glen, giving it back to its citizens, in exchange for the dinosaur. Nightshade imagines a partnership with the shady gambler. Crusader hands Seymour over, aware the creature's voice has gone sour. But the papers are signed. Seeing their fortune disappear, the villains set Seymour free.

Crusader Rabbit in The Yukon Adventure (20 episodes). *Thar's Gold in Them Thar Fills* (one-hour movie format). Residents of the United States are suffering from toothaches at an alarming rate because of a shortage in dental gold used for fillings. Crusader and Rags investigate and discover the major suppliers are located in Ifanyonecan, Yukon. A shadowy scoundrel there has been stealing the precious metal. Crusader and Rags intend to find and recover it. Piloting our heroes to the frozen reaches of Alaska is Dudley Nightshade and Bilious Greene. The villains, both saying they are reformed, want to discover where the gold is so they can steal it for themselves. Several mishaps occur, such as a plane crash, an avalanche, and capture by hostile Eskimos. Crusader, Rags, and the two criminals brave the elements and eventually all make it to the Yukon. The town is rife with lawlessness. Crusader becomes wanted by the law, accused of being the gold thief, when Nightshade and Greene set him up. Will Crusader be vindicated and stop the true thieves, allowing dentists to get their gold to remedy all of the toothaches?

Crusader Rabbit in The Tales of Schmerwood Forest (20 episodes). *Crook's Tour* (one-hour movie format). Trouble is brewing near Galahad Glen, in the adjacent territory of Schmerwood Forest. Robin Hoodlum and his nasty henchmen, Al Catraz and Sam Quentin have a twisted way of robbing from the middle-class and keeping it for themselves. They take Garfield Groundhog hostage and issue a ransom for his safe return. Crusader and Rags disguise themselves as bandits and infiltrate the band. Welcomed into Robin Hoodlum's gang, they begin work on sabotaging their criminal activity. But Rags encounters an accident and

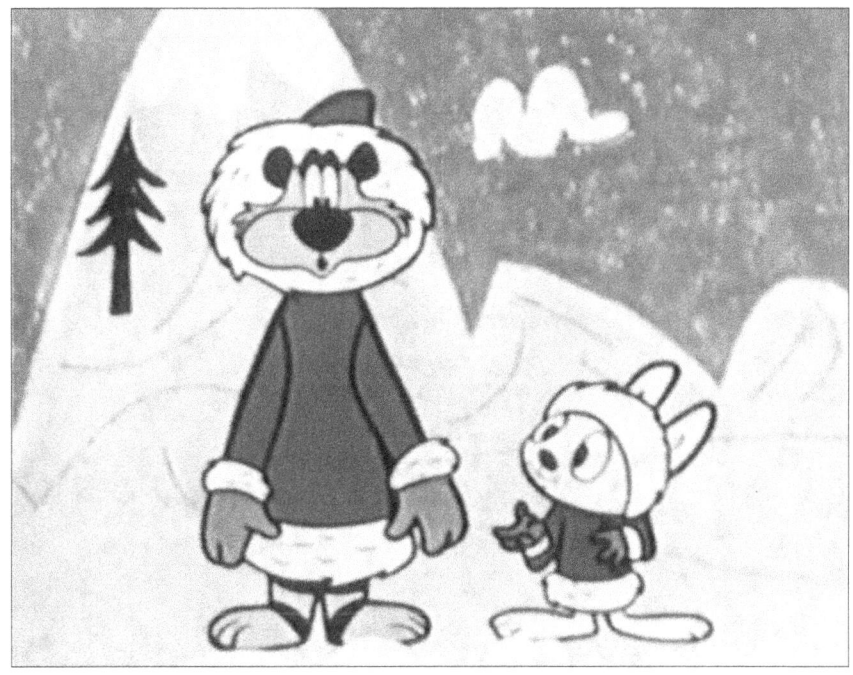

A scene from *Crusader Rabbit in The Yukon Adventure.*

55

suffers from amnesia, and is convinced he is an authentic member of Robin's gang. How long can Crusader keep up the charade before Rags regains his senses or turns his pal in as an imposter?

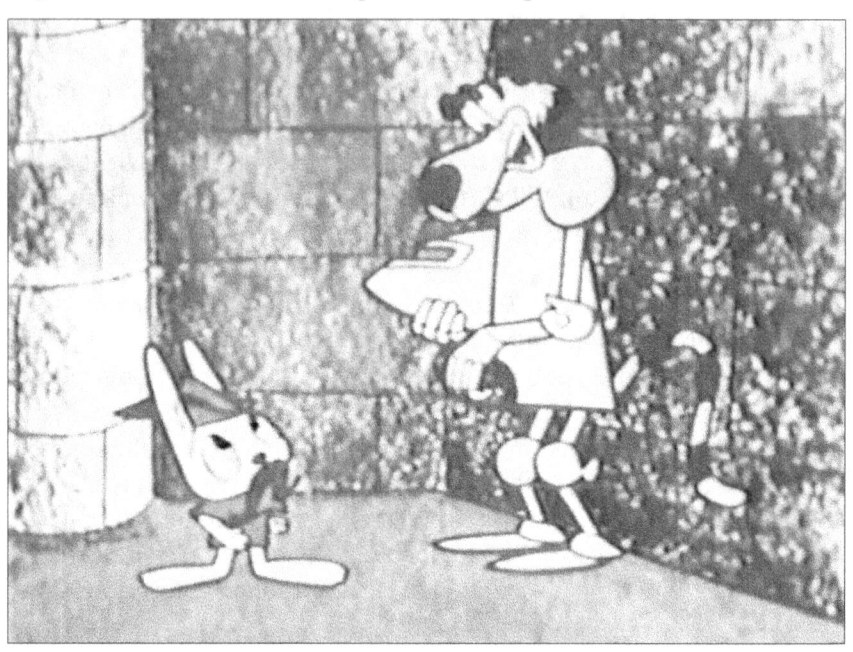

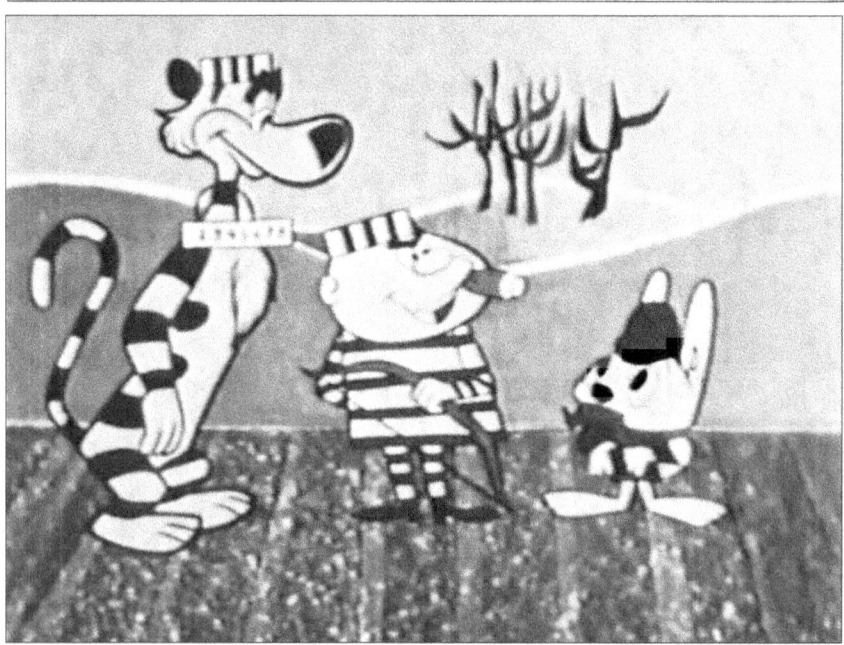

Scenes from *Crusader Rabbit in The Tales of Schmerwood Forest.*

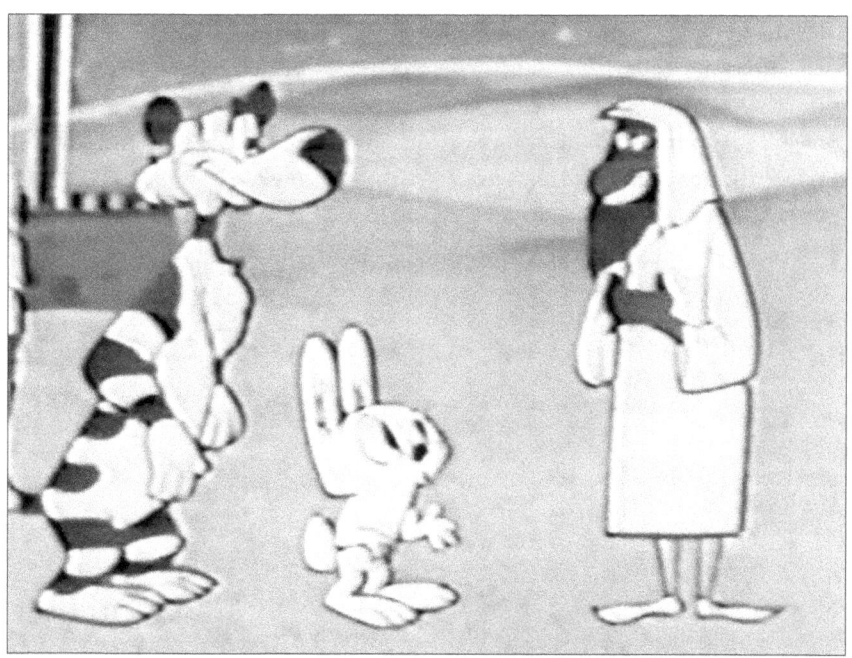

A scene from *Crusader Rabbit in Sahara You.*

Crusader Rabbit in Sahara You (20 episodes). Ragland T. Tiger causes havoc in peaceful Galahad Glen when he breaks a magic Arabian hourglass, causing all citizens to fall under a spell. The only remedy is to replace the sand in the hourglass, which will restore the town. Crusader and Rags journey to the Sahara Desert in search of a remote, mystical area to find the sacred sand. Dudley Nightshade follows, as he wants to get some of the sand, too. With it, he believes, he will rule and control Galahad Glen. The area proves to be hostile. The hare and tiger confront Moe Hamett, guardian of the sacred sands, whose job is to keep infidels away. Crusader and Rags take refuge in Fort Ve-Ate, an abandon Foreign Legion post. But Hamett isn't the only obstacle, Nightshade is too, in disguise. Can Crusader bring some of the magical sand back home and save Galahad Glen?

Crusader Rabbit in West We Forget (20 episodes). Dr. Frank N. Stein, who lives in a mountain-top hideaway, Withering Heights, isn't happy about what's going on below. All of the noise coming out of the little western community of Loudmouth, Wyoming, has distracted his work. While visiting the town, Stein overhears Sheriff Manny Oakley, the town's toughest cowboy, state that only an Indian uprising would quiet things down. Stein assembles a radio-controlled tribe of wooden cigar store Indians on roller skates, with intentions of attacking Loudmouth. Stein captures and locks Rags up. Crusader rescues him. Then Crusader and Rags attempt to warn the town of the invasion. They learn that to be believable they must become tough cowboys, too. Oakley doesn't take kindly to the competition. The heroes encounter and escape several threats. But can they save the town in time?

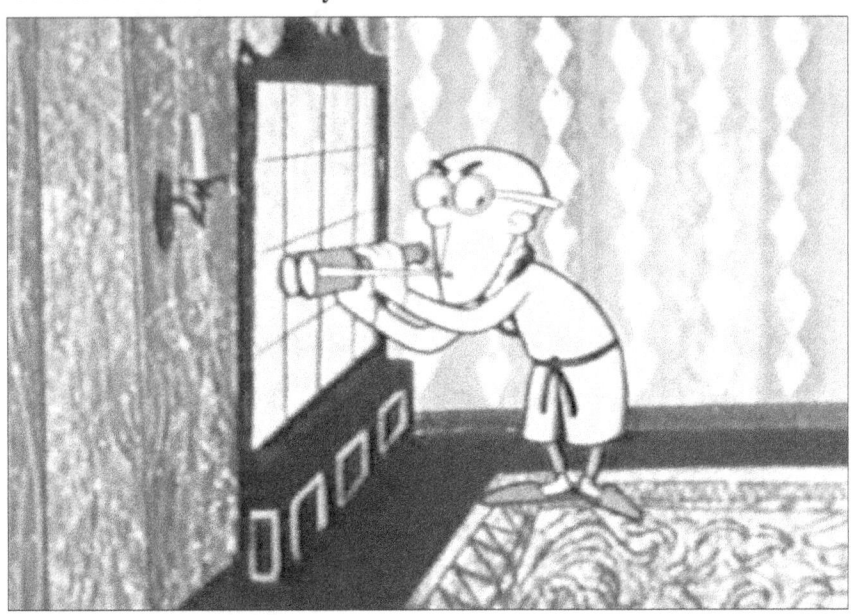

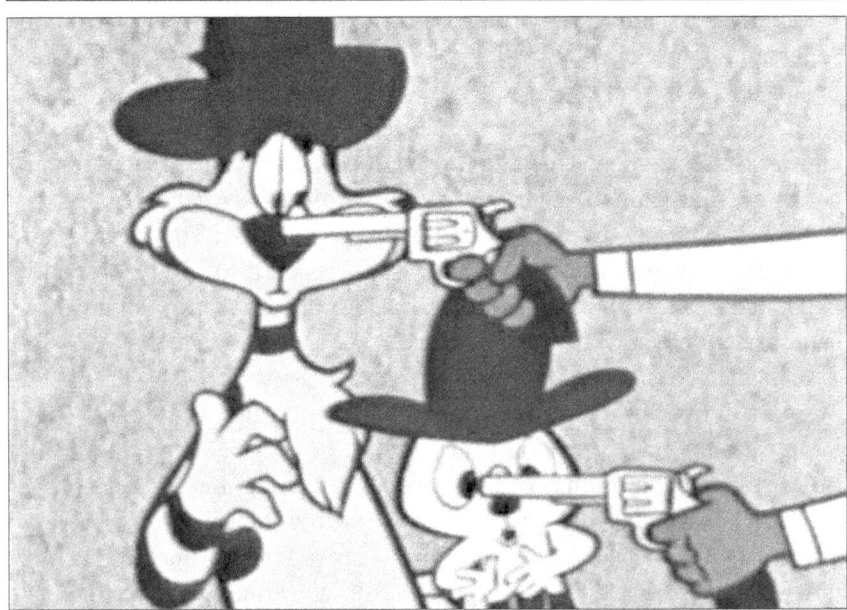

Scenes from *Crusader Rabbit in West We Forget.*

Crusader Rabbit in Gullible's Travels (20 episodes). Professor Ed Foo Yung, a nuclear physicist, and inventor of Chinese Checkers, is held prisoner by Fooey Manchu and his sidekick, King Kong Wong. Crusader and Rags are dispatched by the Pentagon to Red China to investigate. The heroes journey to the ancient temple on the Yangtze, guarded by

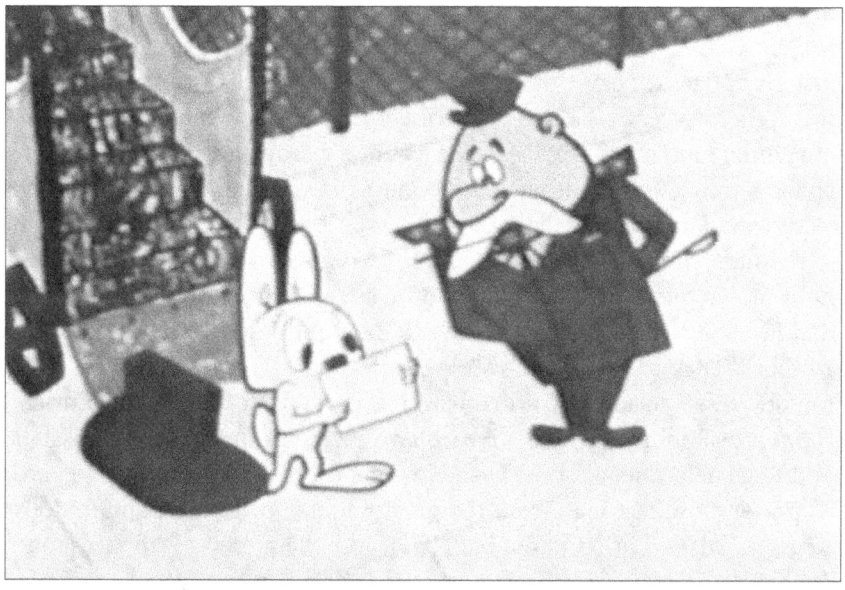

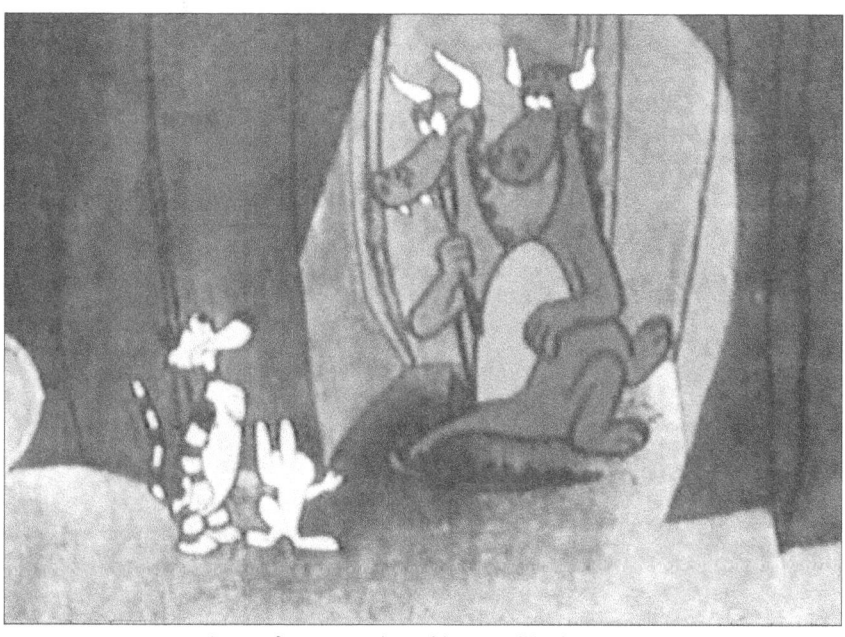

Scenes from *Crusader Rabbit in Gullible's Travels.*

the two-headed dragon, Arson and Sterno. The dragon becomes an ally after the villains try to cheat him out of his pay.

Crusader Rabbit in Should Auld Acquaintance be for Cotton (20 episodes). All of the rivers in America are becoming drained, and Crusader and Rags investigate. Behind the disaster is the gorgeous, but deadly Southern belle Simone Legree, who has hired Dudley Nightshade and Bilious Green. They are using giant, water absorbing Sponge Fish to achieve the task. Legree's objective is to pave over all of the rivers, turning them into roads, so she can strike it rich selling white paint used to create the lane lines. Our heroes encounter many dangers in China, including trying to outrun a rocket. Can Crusader and Rags restore the waterways and stop the diabolical plan?

Crusader Rabbit in Two on the Isle (20 episodes). *Nothing Atoll* (one hour movie format). A ferry veers off course due to a mysterious fog in San Francisco, compelling Crusader Rabbit and Rags to investigate in a rowboat. They are lost in the strange cloud and become castaways on a remote desert island known as Nothing Atoll. There they meet Enrico, the son of Robinson Crusoe. He's busy looking for a treasure. Crusader and Rags help uncover the chest. Now the trio has to protect and guard it, preserving the cache from the greedy hands of pirate Captain Jolly Roger, Cutlass Carl, Cannonball Paul and their crew. Will Crusader,

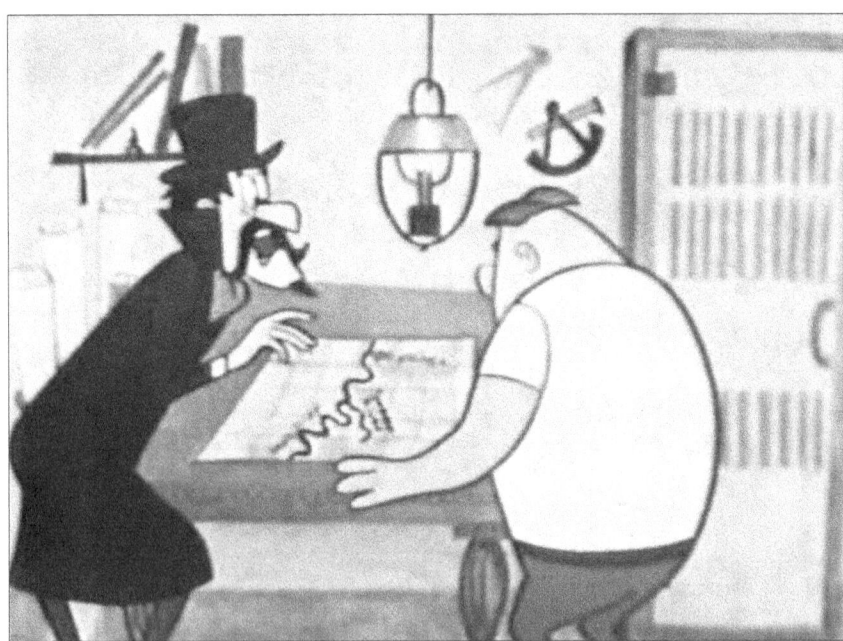

A scene from *Crusader Rabbit in Should Auld Acquaintance be for Cotton.*

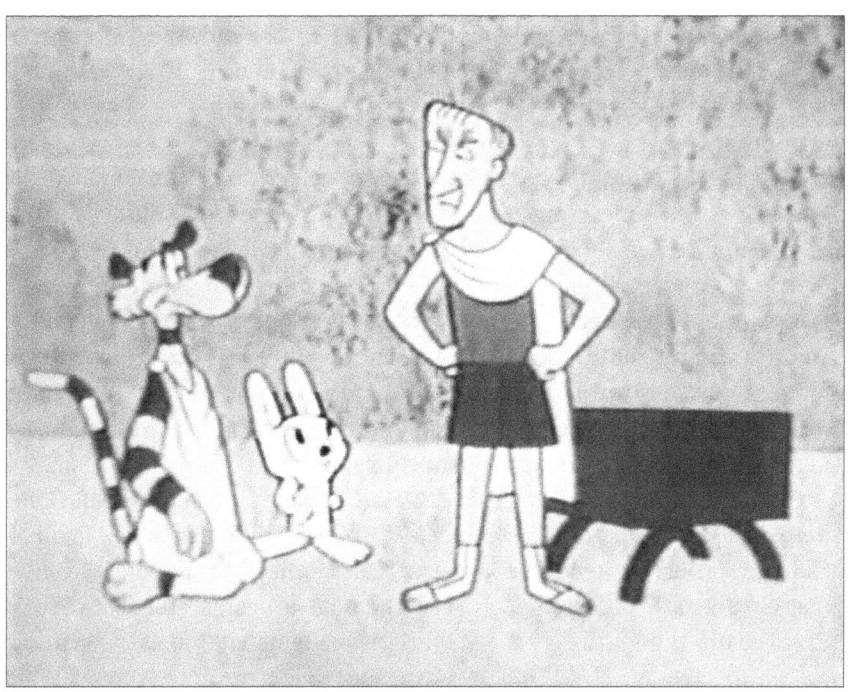

A scene from *Crusader Rabbit in There's No Place Like Rome.*

Rags, and Enrico keep the treasure from falling into Roger's hands?

Crusader Rabbit in Scars and Stripes (20 episodes). Four con men establish The National Holiday Society, to create new holidays. They announce Ragland T. Tiger Week, causing suspicion with Crusader Rabbit. The National Holiday Society has informed citizens the way they can celebrate is by sending them donations that week. But donors are confused and mail the donations directly to Rags in Galahad Glen. The hero hare decides all of the money must be returned to the citizens. The Society's founders, Wearmouth, Chiselhurst, Snidewell and Titus Canby, are determined to get the cash away from them before they can return it. Can Crusader foil the thieves and put an end to the fund-raising, false holidays?

Crusader Rabbit in The Apes of Wrath (20 episodes). Big game hunter, Claude Beauty, enlists the help of Crusader and Rags to go on a safari with him in the Congo. A large cash prize will go to anyone who can photograph the mysterious apes of Wrath, who dwell near a lost temple. The jungle isn't the only challenge facing the team. An active volcano looms, and hostile pygmies are everywhere. The apes aren't the only thing hard to find. The photos snapped of the creatures are mysteriously stolen. Behind the theft is Dudley Nightshade and Bilious

Greene, who have been stalking the troupe. In the end, the secret mystery of the apes is exposed. Their bellies light up and read "Eat at Joe's." The entire mission turns out to be a massive advertising ploy for the restaurant.

Crusader Rabbit in There's No Place Like Rome (20 episodes). *Caesar's Salad* (one-hour movie format). This adventure all takes place in a dream Ragland T. Tiger is having. He dreams he and Crusader Rabbit are in Ancient Rome, as gladiators in a colosseum, winning a race. Impressed by their victory, Emperor Caesar appoints them as his bodyguards. When Caesar is killed, Crusader and Rags are framed by Brutus for his murder. Brutus sells the hare and tiger into slavery. They are rescued from bondage by Nero. But a new danger looms with the burning of Rome. Can they escape the burning city before Rags awakens?

Crusader Rabbit in The Great Baseball Mystery (20 episodes). *Gone with the Wind-Up* (one-hour movie format). The citizens of Galahad Glen are proud of their baseball team. But Dudley Nightshade and Bilious Greene are determined to see them lose against the New York Crankees in the Out of This World Series. Nightshade does everything he can to sabotage the game, but Crusader and Rags enter the stadium and join their team to ensure it doesn't happen. Nightshade's tricks in-

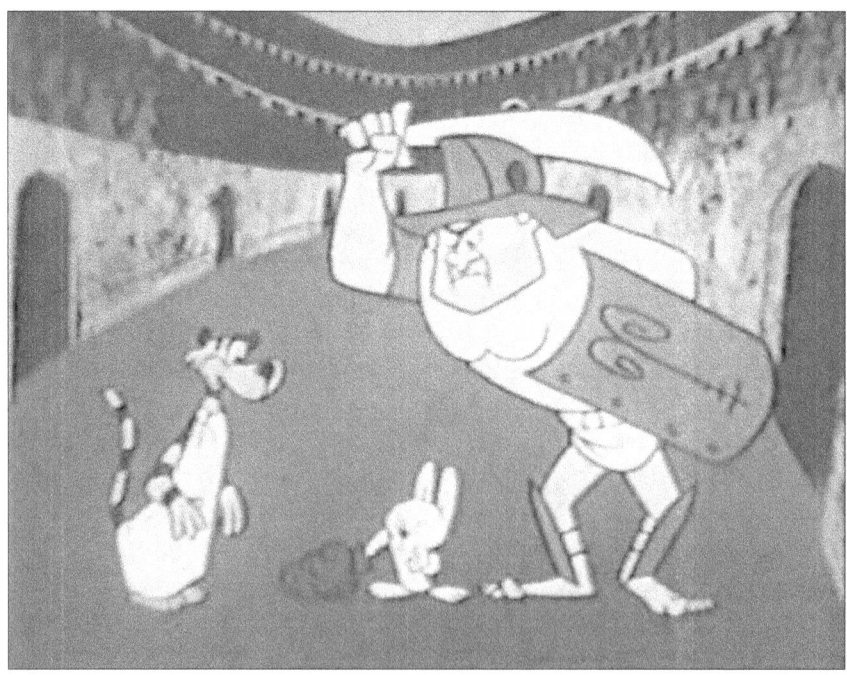

A scene from *Crusader Rabbit in There's No Place Like Rome.*

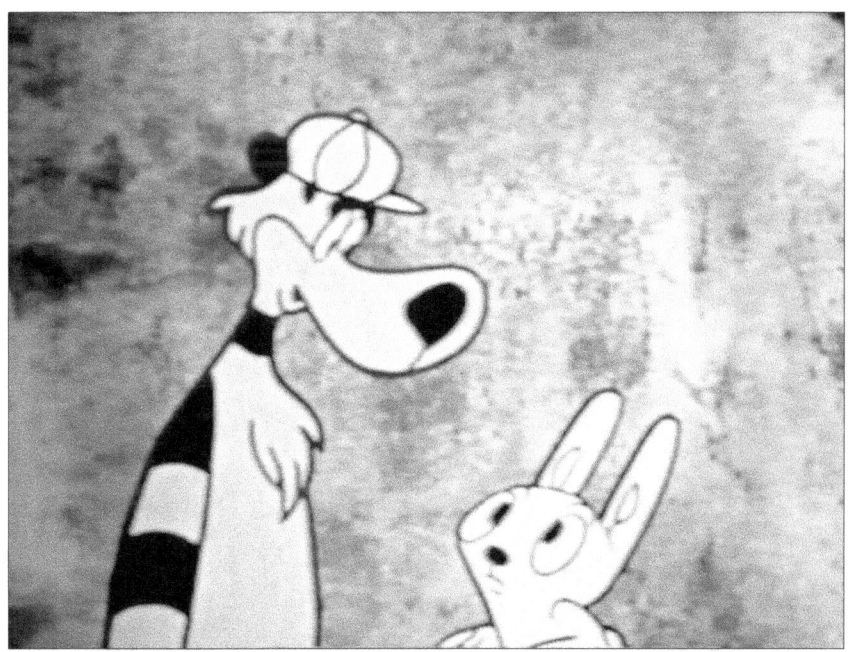

A scene from *Crusader Rabbit in The Great Baseball Mystery.*

clude placing an exploding bat into Rags' hands. But the Galahad Glen team wins. Nightshade abducts their pitcher, Carl Bearstein, and kidnaps the heroes, figuring if he gets rid of them, their team will be the winner next time. The hare and tiger escape, then free Bearstein, who has been hypnotized, becoming a ballet dancer. The heroes face further challenges, including surviving an exploding rocket, and a close call with hungry piranhas. They return, rejoining the Galahad baseball team, and resume their winning streak. Nightshade and his sidekick become a side attraction at the games, where patrons can throw a ball at them and win a prize.

Crusader Rabbit in The Search for the Missing Links (20 episodes). Scotland's Puttingwell Green golf course becomes a hazardous, and spooky place, for golfers. It's littered with booby traps and is said that a sea monster lurks in nearby Veronica Lake. Also, someone has stolen the 18th hole on the course. Golf tournament official Sandy McTraps summons Crusader and Rags to investigate. They face many dangers while snooping around and discover the secret behind the monster of Veronica Lake. Does anyone have a guess? Dudley Nightshade, perhaps?

When TV Spots' vice president and general manager resigned the end of January 1959, *Broadcasting* magazine reported on February 2 that Bob Ganon was promoted to fill the position. Ganon previously had

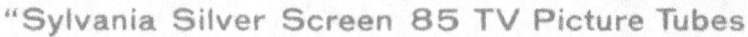
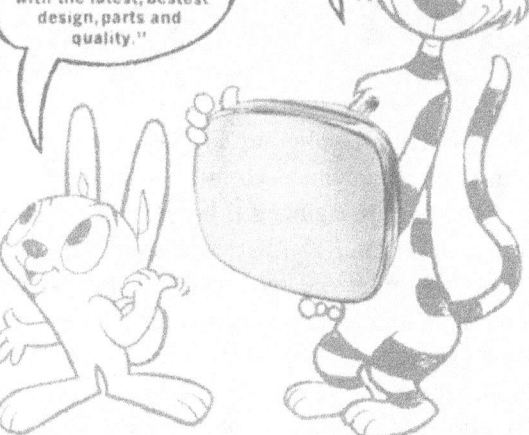
Crusader Rabbit and Rags, with Arthur Godfrey, selling Sylvania television sets.

served as production coordinator for the company.

A surge of new made-for-TV cartoons soon overshadowed the second *Crusader Rabbit* series. Although it performed well out of the gate, Hanna Barbera, along with Jay Ward Productions, was capturing all of the attention.

Jay Ward's *Rocky and Bullwinkle and Friends* gained an enormous amount of publicity prior to its broadcast debut on November 19, 1959.

Essentially the ghost of Television Arts Productions Inc. was back to haunt Bonsall.

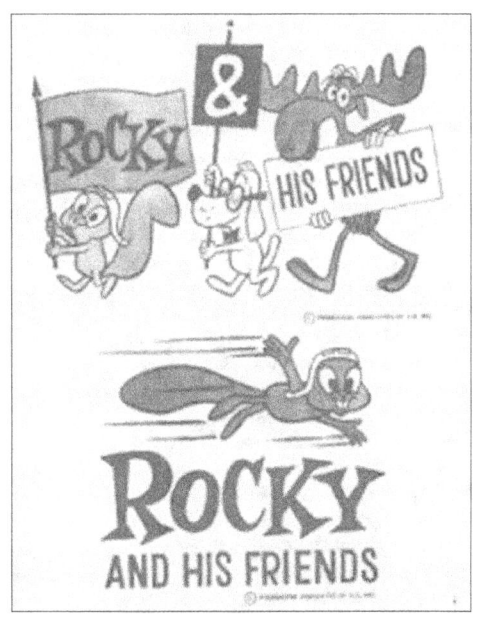

Jay Ward Studios' *Rocky and Bullwinkle.*

TAP vice president of merchandising, R. L. Nunn, responded with anger to an April 11, 1959 article in *Sponsor* about Hanna Barbera's *Huckleberry Hound* being the pioneer program of TV cartoons.

"I want to take particular exception to a sentence you used in your March 28 issue, 'so far *Huckleberry Hound* is the only cartoon series to have been fully created and produced expressly for television.' Our *Crusader Rabbit* was the pioneer in the field," Nunn stated. "It has been on for more than eight years. You reported correctly that sales of the new *Crusader Rabbit* series are over $1.4 million to date."

But not much more.

By 1960, Jay Ward and the squirrel and moose dominated the news concerning animation and broadcast popularity. *Crusader Rabbit* was old news, and anything but new.

But Shull Bonsall already was planning his next big animation thing.

Ever since the live-action *Amos 'n' Andy* TV show ended production in 1953, Bonsall had thought there was something still there to cash in. Thinking of the future for TV Spots, Bonsall approached the show creators, Freeman Gosden and Charles Correll, with an idea.

As the story goes, Bonsall suggested an animated cartoon using their *Amos 'n' Andy* characters as animals, thus avoiding any racial component. Gosden and Correll liked the idea, but demanded complete and

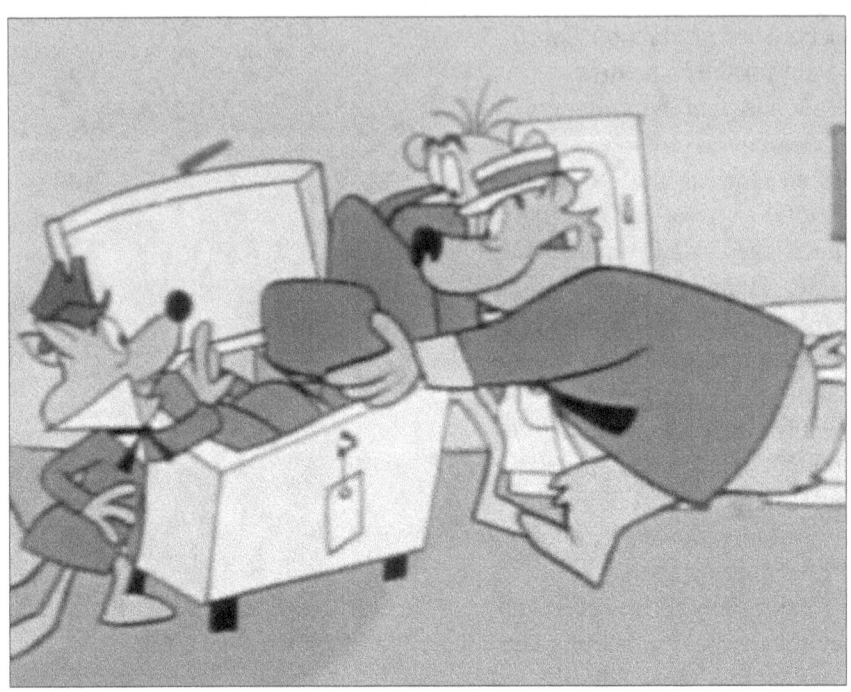
A scene from *Calvin and the Colonel*, 1961.

unfettered creative control over the show. They got it. TV Spots subsequently produced the cartoon, *Calvin and the Colonel,* for one season only, in color.

Calvin and the Colonel represents a moment of justice for Alexander Anderson. He stated later in life that *Calvin and the Colonel* lost Bonsall all of the money he had made on *Crusader Rabbit.*

Later, Bonsall tried to rescue TV Spots by partnering with King Features to create cartoons featuring *Beetle Bailey,* but continued to lose money. TV Spots decided to close its doors to avoid the embarrassment of bankruptcy.

Reportedly, Bonsall once told comics and anime historian, Fred Patten, "I had got my start by buying companies that had gone bankrupt for their assets. So I had no trouble recognizing bankruptcy when it was headed right towards me."

In 1965, Shull Bonsall sold the rights to *Crusader Rabbit,* and the first and second series of films, to Wolper Television Series. It was then acquired by Metromedia Producers Corporation, in 1969, when it took over Wolper Television Series.

In 1982, Metromedia was working on a presentation to pitch to the networks for an all-new *Crusader Rabbit* TV series for the heralded Saturday morning time slot. The preparation originated in a brand-new studio, Cinemation, which was established just for this purpose.

Cinemation was headed up by Lee Orgel, who had worked as producer on the second *Crusader Rabbit* series created by TV Spots.

The staff included Gerry Ray, Sam Nicholson, and Norm Gottfredson.

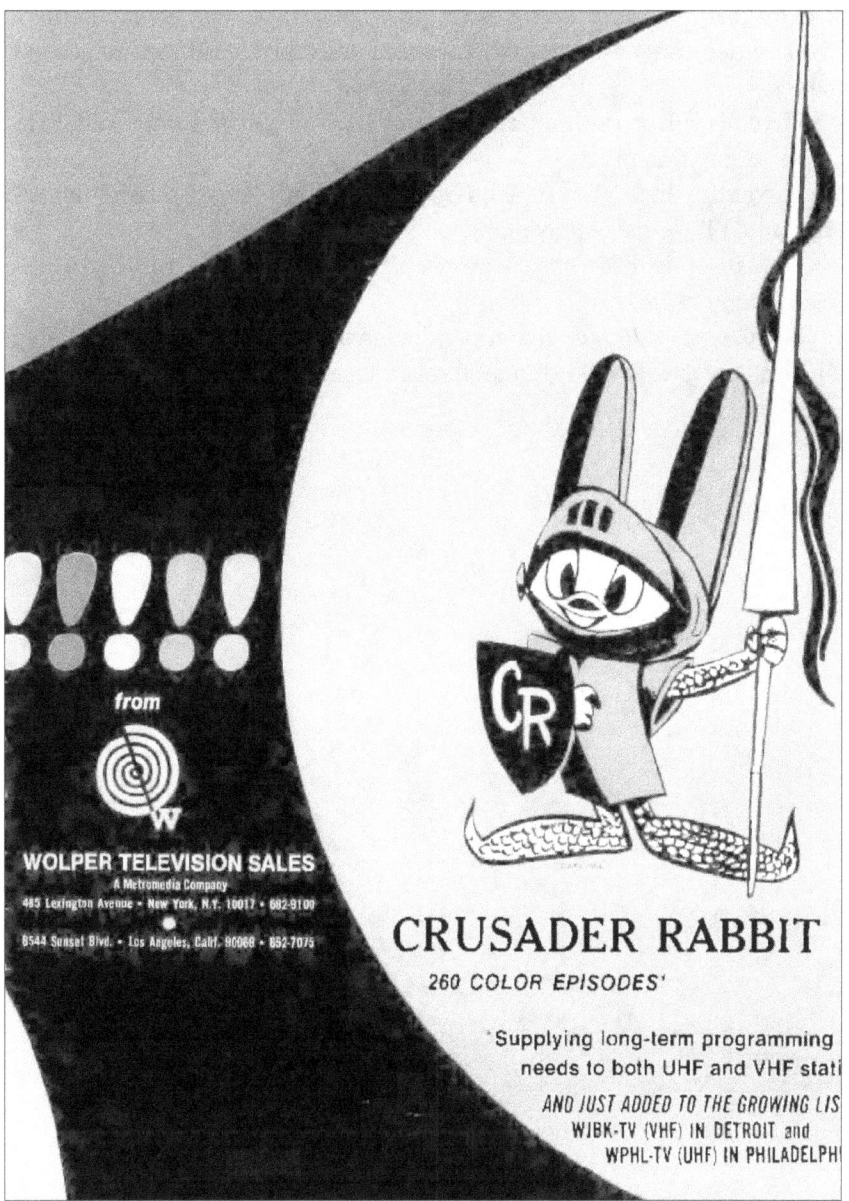

from

WOLPER TELEVISION SALES
A Metromedia Company
485 Lexington Avenue • New York, N.Y. 10017 • 682-9100
8544 Sunset Blvd. • Los Angeles, Calif. 90069 • 652-7075

CRUSADER RABBIT

260 COLOR EPISODES'

`Supplying long-term programming
needs to both UHF and VHF stati

AND JUST ADDED TO THE GROWING LIS
WJBK-TV (VHF) IN DETROIT and
WPHL-TV (UHF) IN PHILADELPH

Wolper Television Sales ad, pitching *Crusader Rabbit* to TV stations.

All had previously worked on the 1950's animated adventures of *Crusader Rabbit*. However, a new series never surfaced.

In 1985, Metromedia sold the character and both film series to 20th Century Fox.

In 2009, ATI (Audio Tape Incorporated) released a 3-disc DVD collection featuring *Crusader Rabbit*, presenting two complete adventures from series one, and material from nine tales produced for the second series.

Virtually all of the material on the DVD originated from old VHS tapes, not 35mm prints.

Currently, there are no plans by 20th Century Fox to reissue the series on DVD, or make it available on streaming video.

The tale of the little hero, who stood two-and-a-half carrots high, officially came to an end.

But *Crusader Rabbit* remains popular today, and historic, for being the first created-for-TV animated cartoon series.

CHAPTER FIVE

Other Crusader Adventures

Toys come and go, but adventures are here to stay. Aside from the animated cartoon series, there are only four other Crusader Rabbit stories that were released, all appearing in print books.

Two comic books were published by Dell, *Four Color* #735 (October 1956), and *Four Color* #805 (May 1957). There were two story books published, *Crusader Rabbit Wonder Book* #698, released by Classic Enterprises Inc. (1958), and *Crusader Rabbit in Bubble Trouble*, released by Whitman Publishing Company (1960).

The two Dell comic books presented stories based on the animated cartoon series. So, the adventures were not new.

Four Color #735, written by Nancy Hoag and illustrated by Dan Gormley, presents two stories. In the first tale, *The Schmohawk Indians*, a native tribe kidnaps Rags. Crusader Rabbit rescues him and persuades the Schmohawks that they can become famous by going on the warpath. The Schmohawks get captured by Babyface Barracuda and his gang, who steal their clothes and dress as Schmohawks when they rob a bank. In the second tale, *Leprechaun's Gold*, Crusader Rabbit and Rags are made honorary leprechauns. All the leprechauns have to hide the pots of gold that follow them. Rags drops his pot down a hole that is

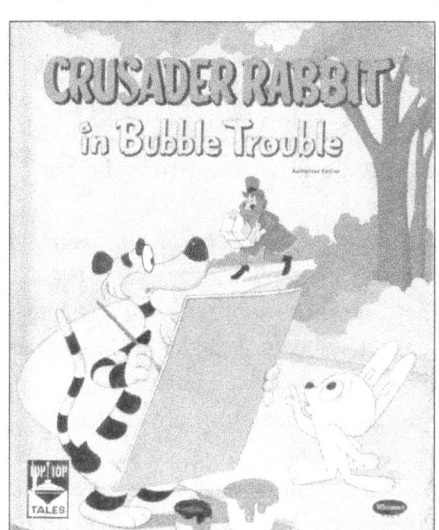 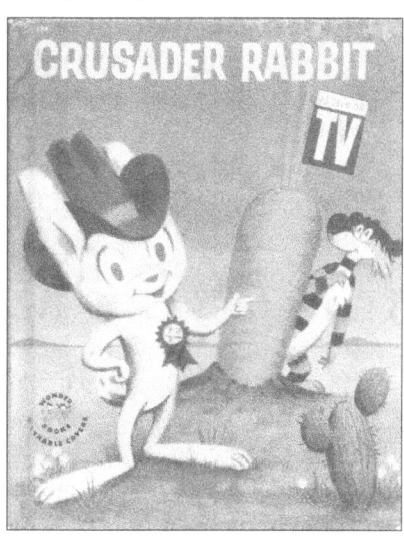

Crusader Rabbit books, *Bubble Trouble* and *Wonder Book*.

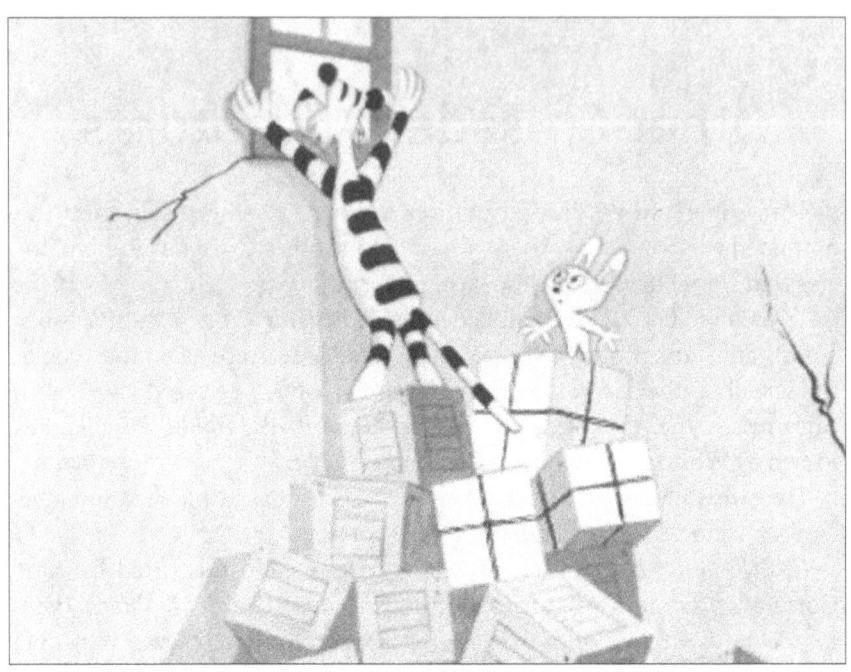

A scene from *Bubble Trouble*.

the home of Garfield Groundhog. Garfield goes on a spending spree that sets off a gold rush. To help settle the damage, Crusader and Rags must go to Ireland and get fast-growing, hollow oak acorns from Finn McCool, the forty-foot giant.

Four Color #805, written by Nancy Hoag and illustrated by Dan Gormley, presents two stories. In the first tale, *The Tenth Century*, Crusader and Rags step through a magic mirror and find themselves back in Medieval times. In the second tale, *The Circus Mystery*, Crusader and Rags try to rescue the circus where Rags once lived.

Nancy Hoag, a teacher turned prolific author, also wrote the 1960 Crusader Rabbit picture book, *Bubble Trouble*.

Bubble Trouble was illustrated by Whitman and Golden Books' artist, Jan Neely. While Bob Bemiller is listed as an illustrator, Neely created the art. Bemiller, director of animation on the second *Crusader Rabbit* series, worked with Neely using model sheets in order to have the series' characters appear identical to their animated adventures.

In the book, Crusader Rabbit and Rags start a super delivery service. Their first customer is Dudley Nightshade, who is in disguise and not recognized by our heroes. Nightshade leaves them a package to be delivered on Ghost Road to Mrs. Bud. They arrive at a haunted house on a cliff and meet Mrs. Bud, who turns out to be Robin Hoodlum in dis-

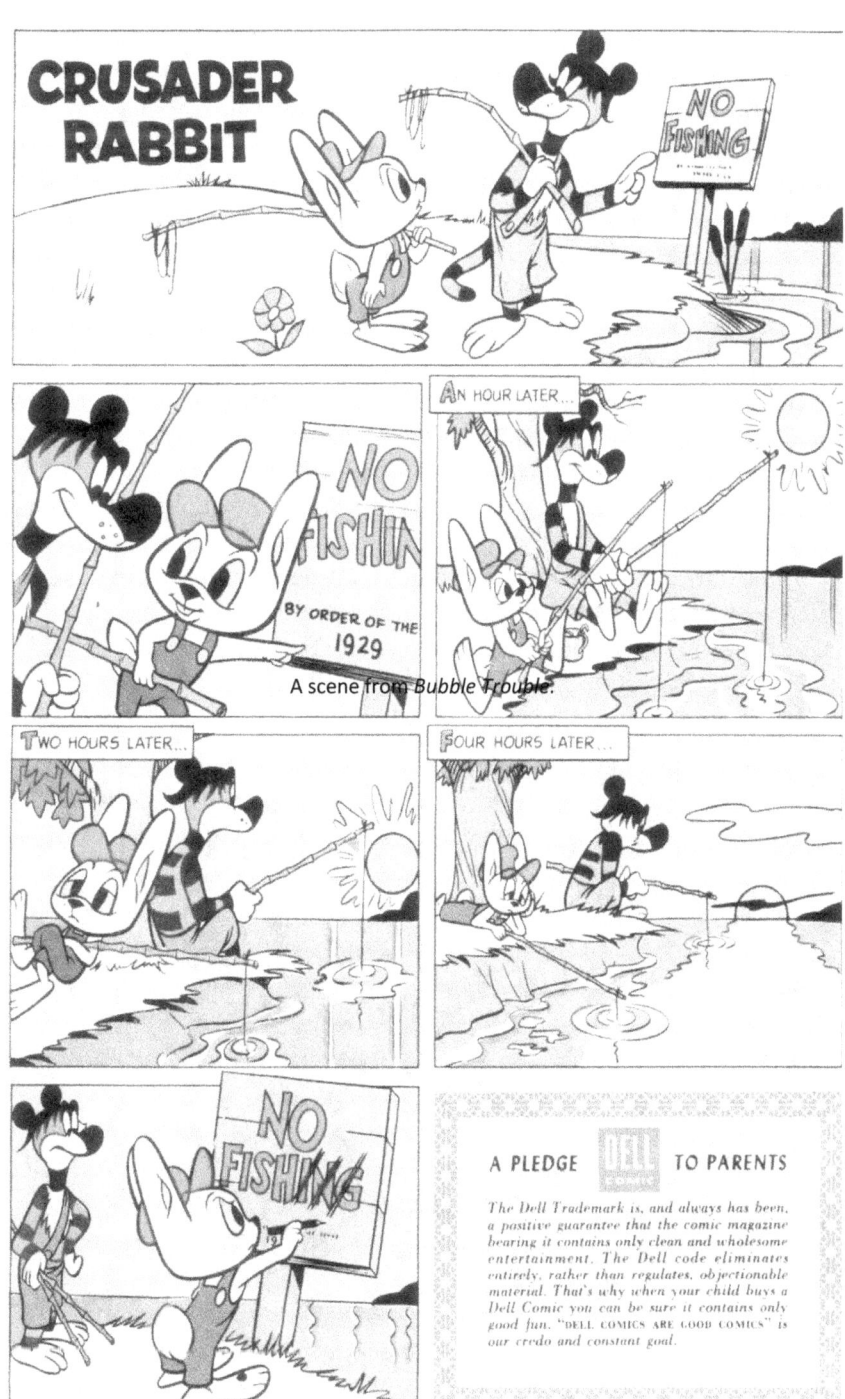

A scene from *Bubble Trouble*.

A Dell comic book page.

guise. His associates, Al Catraz, Sam Quinten, Bulgy Bill and Nightshade, capture Crusader and Rags, locking them in a storeroom. The heroic hare blows a huge bubblegum bubble, lifting out the window. The crooks are arrested and jailed. The major gives Crusader and Rags a reward for the apprehension of the criminals.

The *Crusader Rabbit Wonder Book*, written by Oscar Weigle and illustrated by Arthur Kruse, presents a variation of the first Crusader Rabbit animated cartoon adventure, *Crusader Rabbit vs. the State of Texas*. The delightful tale about a deportation for rabbits to the North Pole. And their return.

Arthur Krusz didn't draw Crusader Rabbit and Rags identical to their animated appearance, but provided a whimsical feel to the colorful art. Krusz had become a professional illustrator based in New York a few years previously, and created elaborate sci-fi illustrations for popular fiction magazines.

Thus, only *Bubble Trouble* presents an all-new Crusader Rabbit story, not based on an adventure from the cartoon series. However, the other tales do vary slightly from their film presentations.

The books are still available and highly collectible, and generally reasonably priced, depending on condition.

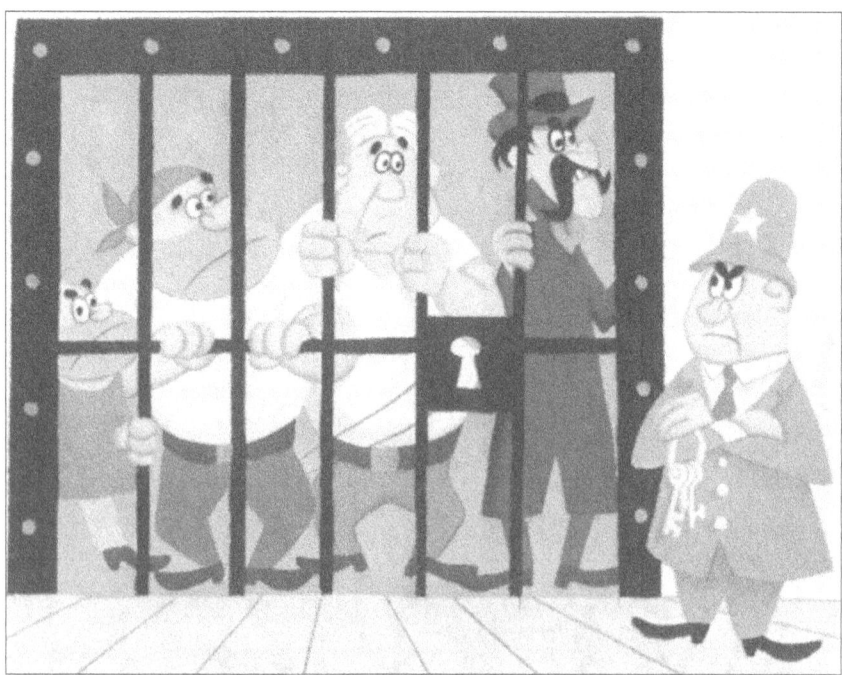

A scene from *Bubble Trouble*.

.

www.ingramcontent.com/pod-product-compliance
Lightning Source LLC
Chambersburg PA
CBHW071231220526
45468CB00002B/803